Introduction.

Are you someone who likes surprises? Are you someone who likes suspense? I am NOT! As incredible as surprises are, if I even get a clue that a surprise is going to happen, I get really nervous. I'm the weirdo who likes to know how books and movies are going to end before I dive into them. I don't need to know the exact ending every time. But I do want to know if there is a happy ending or a sad ending. I'm going to go on the journey either way, I just need to brace myself for the feelings that are about to happen.

I feel like a lot of people are like that. They want to know what they are getting into before they go down the road of surprise and suspense. So, I am going to start by telling you the end. I am going to start by admitting that some of these stories and lessons are hard for me to write about. Some of them might even be hard for you to read. I just want to assure you that THIS story has a happy ending. It has one of the most beautiful and happy ending you could ever imagine.

Thank you so much for being willing to go on this journey with me. It hasn't been an easy one. Probably much like yours, it's had its challenges at each level. But it's been worth it. Your journey will be worth it also. It takes courage to live a life full of lessons. I have that courage. You have that courage.

If you have ever thought about writing a book but are hesitant, reach out to me. Let's have a conversation. I want to encourage and cheer for you. Writing this book has been such a magical and freeing experience for me. It's been a living and breathing thing from the start. I never knew how many stories I had to tell until I started outlining the chapters. There's something freeing and exciting about sharing all of these lessons with others in the form of a book. It's also been oddly therapeutic. For so long, I didn't understand why certain things happened the way they did in my life. Putting all of the lessons and experiences together in this format has given me so much peace and clarity. It can be the same for you if you have the courage to share your story.

The rough start that I am so grateful for.

If you could go back and change ANYTHING in your life, what would you change?

As a mom, it breaks my heart the way my parents raised me and my brother. While I am not quite ready to talk about all of it, I feel like it's important to share as much as I can with you. I don't share these stories so that you will feel sorry for me. On the contrary, I tell these stories and share my life with you so that you see what's possible. I share my experiences so you can see how tough situations make us tougher. I share my experiences with you so you can see that each difficult situation offers us a lesson and a new way of looking at things if we let it.

Growing up, my life was less than ideal. Yeah. Let's call it that.

I basically grew up on the corner of poverty and dysfunction. That's right. I said it. Much like everything else in my life, it helped shape me but it certainly doesn't define me.

Let's start with two parents that wanted to pretend they didn't have children. They divorced early and then shuffled my brother and me back and forth from city to city, like a twisted game of "you're it." We lived with the "it" parent for a few years, and then it was time to be shuffled back to the other parent. We never felt like we had a choice. One day, it was just time to pack up our stuff and go live with the other parent. There was never any tears of being sad to leave one parent. It was just what happened every few years. In a twisted way, my brother and I got used to it and just accepted it as normal.

I'll never forget the time when I was twelve and my mom bought us one-way bus tickets to go visit our dad. He thought we were coming for a two-week visit. Boy, was he surprised. My mom basically told us before she put us on the bus that she didn't want us around anymore. She told us that maybe after a few years, we could come back. As a mom, I can't even begin to understand how you can send your children away, but I sure remember how it made me feel at that age. Being shipped back and forth like that made us feel worthless and unloved. It's still hard to think about even though I can appreciate how much I have grown from it.

Our parents always lived in different states. There was none of this visiting on weekends like what happens with a lot of parents now. When we didn't live with that specific parent, we didn't visit them. There was no seeing both of our parents on a regular basis. Whichever parent didn't have us got to pretend they didn't have kids. They got to pretend for a time that we didn't exist.

When I was in kindergarten, we lived with my dad and his 2nd wife in Oklahoma City. They had been married for a few years and had beautiful wedding pictures displayed in their house. One picture in particular always caught my attention. It was of my dad's wife in her big white wedding dress. She was sitting in the grass. The dress was spread out all around her. She had a least 6 or 7 small kids sitting on the dress around her. Everyone was looking up and smiling. They looked so happy. One day, in all of my six-year-old braveness, I finally asked the question that I had been wanting to ask for a long time. "Why wasn't I invited to your wedding?" I don't remember the answer, but I do remember the sadness I felt as a tiny little girl knowing that I wasn't even important enough to be invited to my own father's wedding.

One household wasn't any better than the other. Both were filled with deep negativity, constant manipulation, and the occasional episode of mental and physical abuse. Neither one of my parents figured out how to be in a loving partnership of marriage. All they seemed to jump into were dysfunctional relationships that brought them ZERO amounts of joy. When you don't have joy in your heart, you can't give joy to others. Not even your children.

And you know what? I'm grateful for all of it.

One of the most difficult things I've lived through happened when I was sixteen. My dad and I lived in a tiny little apartment. He'd already ruined things with his third wife. He had used her up and spit her out. She finally got tired of taking care of everyone and working two jobs to pay all the bills. She wised up and left him. My brother had already moved out on his own. He escaped when he was seventeen by getting a job and moving in with some friends. I wasn't quite that lucky yet. My dad decided nothing was worth living for and tried to commit suicide – "tried" being the key word here. This attempt left him with months and months of hospitalization and a liver transplant.

Now, at sixteen, you don't really understand mental struggles like that. So, the message I received was that *I* wasn't worth living for.

You think I'm upset all of that happened? No way! It was one of the most emotionally gut-wrenching things I have ever gone through. That one decision my father made sent my life in a downward spiral for the next three years. It left emotional scars that will never heal. I never complained and I never played the victim. In fact, I'm grateful for it.

Surprisingly, I'm even grateful that all of the stress brought out a dormant blood-clotting disorder that I had. I was born with it but never knew or experienced any problems. Apparently, I had it all along, but it never "flared up." Because of the tremendous amount of stress in my life, it surfaced and started causing havoc. For the next ten years, I would have countless weeklong hospital stays and numerous procedures and operations to try to prevent my body from randomly creating blood clots in my veins. I still deal with it today and will for the rest of my life. The worst part about all of that was that my parents decided to stay uninvolved with all of the medical trauma. My mom came to visit me in the hospital once. She said she just wanted to make sure I was still alive. My dad never came to visit me. Can you imagine being a seventeen-year-old kid dealing with all of that alone? I didn't understand it then, and I still don't understand it now. That's ok. I was meant to survive and learn from it. I wasn't meant to understand it.

My overall core belief is that people are honestly doing the best job they can with what they have. Are there bad people in the world? Of course! Do I believe my parents were bad people? No way! I believe that, in their own way, they loved me and my brother very much. They honestly did the best job they could and did what they thought was best in the moment. That's what I choose to believe, and I am grateful for all of it.

So why on earth am I so thankful for those experiences, plus the messes that I got my own self into once I was on my own?

Because to change ANYTHING is to change EVERYTHING.

And I would not change my current life for anything.

We want to look at everything in our lives and label it good or bad.

"Oh, I wish that had not happened."

"Oh, I wish I hadn't made that mistake."

"I wish I hadn't done this or that."

But what we forget is that every mistake we make comes with a lesson. Every experience we have, good or bad, leaves an impression on us. It is our choice what impression it leaves. I can easily look back at my childhood, my adolescence, all the mistakes I made in my twenties and my thirties, and say, "I wish I hadn't done all of that. I wish I had been smarter. I wish I had made better decisions." But that's not going to do me any good. I've learned so many incredible lessons through my "failures." Every experience has made me a strong, incredible, and capable woman. I wouldn't change anything.

I've been married to my incredible husband for sixteen-plus years. Had I not failed at every single previous relationship, I wouldn't have met him. Even after 18 plus years of being together, I still would rather spend time with him than anyone else. I learned so much about myself through those relationships. The good, the bad, the ugly... the things I needed to fix and the things that I expected from a partner. My beloved husband is truly a saint for putting up with me all these years. I treat him like the treasure he is on a regular basis. Is our marriage perfect? No, but it's really close. We are both quick to acknowledge when we have messed up and work together to make our marriage strong. We are both strong and driven personalities, so conflicts do happen. Funny thing is, I wouldn't want to be married to anyone who wasn't a strong and driven personality. Because of my failed relationships, I am aware of that. And what a blessing it is.

We own a thriving insurance brokerage in Kansas City and have an amazing team. Had I not made mistakes in previous careers, I wouldn't have the knowledge that keeps my business and team moving forward. I am STILL learning how to be a leader and run a business. I have made some bad hires, for sure, but every one of them has brought me closer to the team I have now. I've had some jobs in my life that I didn't love. We all have. Those failed jobs and career moves showed me that one of my priorities is having a business that supports me and my family's lifestyle. I have been in the position where my business owned me and I basically lived to support it. Because I have been in those situations, I run our business a little differently. I make sure it fits into our "Life By Design" philosophy. We have been trapped by our businesses before. Those lessons have been incredible in moving our company forward in a way that it serves us instead of us serving it.

I have two incredible sons, who fill my heart with joy most days. Okay, EVERY day, but some days just a little less joy because they drive me crazy. Can I get an amen from the parents in the room? I have never made a mistake or done anything wrong as a mom. I am the best mom ever! I am joking! I apologize to my kids on a regular basis. Usually, it sounds something like, "Sorry, guys! That did NOT turn out the way I expected." Because I had such a difficult upbringing and poor examples of parents, I don't take my kids for granted. I see them as the gift and treasures they are on a regular basis instead of seeing them as burdens the way my parents did. I remind them daily that it is such a pleasure to be their mom. I tell them at least weekly that I am so thankful that God picked me to be their mom and that I love them so much. No one talked to me like that when I was a kid. And that's ok. I have decided that cycle ends with me. My boys are growing up in a home that shows love, support, and encouragement no matter what. Even when we make mistakes or they let their standards start to slip, we work together to get back on track. Because we are a team. Team Stroud sticks together. All for one. One for all.

I'm a runner and an adventure junkie who gets to travel on a regular basis. Yes. Even during a pandemic, I travel on a regular basis. Each adventure teaches me a little more about myself. I've had numerous injuries to my hands, knees, and feet because of the running and adventures, but I wouldn't change any of it. The occasional pain I feel reminds me I am alive and I am moving my body. Because we didn't live in homes with any kind of standards growing up, I have to put standards on myself. I have to push myself physically to see how far I can go. We didn't play sports or compete in any competitions growing up and I think those things are important. I don't get upset about it. I just make sure that I am putting myself in competitions now so I can improve myself mentally and physically.

If I changed anything about my upbringing or my past mistakes and struggles, I wouldn't have what I have or be everything I am now. So, stop looking backwards and labeling things. Stop looking backwards with regrets and unhappiness. Instead, extract the lessons and keep moving forward because that's the direction you're going.

I have learned so much about myself and the world as a whole through my short forty-two years on this planet. I have made a TON of mistakes. There have been plenty of times when I have had to ask myself really difficult questions. There have been plenty of times when I have been my only cheerleader. There have been times when I have had to give myself pep talks because no one else could understand what I was going through or dealing with.

This book is a collection of all of those wonderful things. I am proud to share my failures and struggles with you because I know it will help a few people. I am proud to tell you all the incredibly stupid things I have done because I know someone is going through the same thing.

Now let's jump into these crazy stories and my crazy journey so I can show you how I went from The Corner of Poverty and Dysfunction to The Lady CEO. It's an incredible journey, and I am so glad you are here to share it with me.

Did you marry a bad decision?

Just because you made a bad decision doesn't mean you have to stay married to it.

Let's talk about this in the most literal sense. When I was twenty, I made the fantastic decision to get married. I'm not a big fan, personally, of people getting married when they're young. What in the world do we know about being married at twenty years old? I barely knew who I was at twenty years old and had no business getting married. But there I was, twenty years old, married, living in a little house with a husband. The only problem was, I didn't know how to be married. I don't think he really knew how to be married either. He had an excellent example of parents and what marriage looks like, but to see something and to do something are two completely different things. And we all know that I didn't have any wonderful examples of marriage in my life. Plus, I had been left behind and abandoned by people who should have been trying to protect me. I was used to fending for myself and doing things on my own. I wasn't in a place, emotionally, where I should have been trying to be a partner to anyone.

I had no idea where I was going in my life or how to get there. I had no idea how to even take care of myself, let alone be a partner or help take care of someone else. I had little to no personal standards for myself and my life, which meant I had little to no standards for the people I allowed into my life.

The really sad part is that I knew before I got married that I shouldn't have done it. There were so many warning signs that he was not ready to be married. There were so many warning signs that he was not the person I wanted to grow old and have children with. But I went through with it because I didn't want to be "that girl" who called off her wedding. I didn't want to be "that girl" who disappointed the families involved and everyone who had put so much work into a wedding.

I guess I hoped things would get better and turn out great. Spoiler alert... They did not! I remember telling a friend, "I don't want to be divorced." I was so upset, but I knew this was not the path I wanted to be on for the rest of my life. I finally made the decision to end the marriage and file for divorce. And guess what? It's not as terrible as you might think. Getting divorced is not the end of the world. As a matter of fact, it was just the beginning of my world. Looking back, it was a difficult decision, but I'm glad I made it. And I'm glad I went through with it.

At that time in my life, the WORST thing I could have done was "stick it out" and hope that things got better. The real mistake would have been putting more time or energy into the relationship. The real mistake would have been continuing down a path I KNEW was not the path I needed to be on. It would have been a real tragedy on many levels to keep running a million miles an hour in a direction that I knew I shouldn't be going in. At one point, I remember him saying to me, "We can go to counseling. YOU can change!" *No. No, I don't think I will. I don't want to change. Here's your sign, Jessica. Here is your sign!*

Why is it that we are so afraid to be wrong?

Why is it that we are so afraid to admit that we have changed our minds?

Why is it that we are so afraid to admit that we made a mistake?

What if you buy a pair of shoes and they don't fit? Maybe they fit great in the store, but you wear them around for a couple of days and they start to really hurt your feet. They start to give you blisters. Would you just keep wearing them? Would you just keep torturing yourself and your feet by wearing the shoes? Or would you toss them aside and get new ones?

What if you buy something at the grocery store and you get it home and it smells terrible? You decide to cook it and eat it anyway because you paid money for it so you can't just let it go to waste. It's rotten and it makes you throw up every time you eat it. Are you still going to keep eating it every single day, day after day? No! You are going to stop eating it.

So, then, why is it that if you get a job or you move to a new position and you know that it's not a good fit, that you don't want to admit it? This happened to me several times around 2011 and 2012 with a company I worked for. They kept "promoting" me and I didn't feel like the promotions were a good fit.

In 2011, I took a job selling marketing for a company out of Alabama. It was a great job. I loved it. The delicate combination of hunting and closing new sales fit my personality very well. The freedom of being an outside salesperson was even better. I got to set my own appointments and keep my own schedule. As long as I was turning in my sales every week, no one bothered me.

My territory was about half of Kansas and half of Missouri. So, I traveled around just a little bit, servicing my accounts and making new calls. Most of the time, I was gone maybe one or two nights a month from home, but it wasn't terrible. Even with my boys being super young, John and I managed because there were so many other benefits to the job. It worked out after about a year. I was doing so well that the manager came to me and said that they wanted me to be the National Sales Trainer for the company. What an honor that was! I couldn't believe it. I was so excited.

The only downfall was it included lots of travel. And when I say lots, I'm talking three to four trips every single month and each trip lasted three or four days. This was way more travel than I expected, and way more than I had ever done before. At first, my manager talked about having all the new hires fly into Kansas City, where I lived, so I could train them in my own territory. That didn't last long. He soon told me he felt like they needed to be trained in their own areas. I think people look at traveling for business as very interesting and romantic until you actually have to do it. Then it just becomes a drag. You get tired of living out of a suitcase. You miss your family. You get tired of eating out and airports. I knew within a few months that this new position was not going to work for me or my family, but I was so scared to say anything. I grew to hate it when the company hired a new salesperson because that just meant more travel for me.

I finally had the courage to be honest with myself and do something about it. After six months or so, I went to my manager and told him I hated it. I didn't want to do it anymore. I was so nervous to tell him; I didn't want to admit that it wasn't a good fit for me. To his credit, he understood and made a suggestion. "How about you become the manager for your territory?" he asked. This meant I would be the sales manager over the territory that I had already been in. That sounded like a great idea! At first.

There are times in my life that I have been EXTREMELY naïve. This was definitely one of them. Did the company have proven systems to follow? Yes. Was the process simple? Yes. But I was incredibly naïve to think that just because you can DO something yourself means you can TEACH others to do it. We all have our own little tweaks and spins we put on things. Even following a proven system, we will bring our own personalities to the mix. I still struggle with the mindset of "Well, if I can do it, ANYONE can do it." I so desperately want that to be true. But it's just not.

Needless to say, that also didn't work out for me. So, again, I had to put my tail between my legs and nervously go to my manager and tell him this was not working for me, and it was not what I wanted to do. He could tell just by looking at my numbers. No one I hired seemed to work out, so I was doing all of the selling myself. Luckily enough, he suggested I take back my territory and do what I did before. I was fortunate enough that I had that opportunity when so many others in this situation might not have. I see it so often in companies where people basically get promoted out of a job. You are doing great, so you get promoted. And on and on until you aren't doing so great anymore. It's sad.

About two years after I started our insurance company, I had the opportunity to expand into other states. Two different gentlemen came to me separately with the same idea. I would open an insurance company in the state that they lived in. They would help provide all of the leads and referrals into the company. They both owned large, well-respected mortgage companies, so this was a big deal. I would just basically have to run it and keep the insurance side of things going smoothly. It sounded like a wonderful idea. I had so much respect for these gentlemen and the fact that they wanted to partner with me meant so much to me. I was so honored. So, for about five months, I started down that path. I started looking at getting licensed in other states, started looking at having different office spaces, and started looking at having different companies in different LLCs and partnerships with these two gentlemen.

I really started down a rabbit hole and almost got myself in too deep. Luckily enough, my husband feels comfortable telling me his opinions. One day, he sat me down and asked, "Are you sure this is a good idea?"

I said, "What do you mean? It's expansion! It's new companies. It's partnerships. It's going to be great. Of course it's a good idea!"

He had the strength to remind me that when somebody quit, I was going to have to fly out to each location to replace them. He also reminded me that when somebody needs to be hired... when somebody needs to meet the reps... when something's not going right... When there's licensing... when there's interviewing... who's going to do all that? Who's going to oversee all of the policies and the procedures for these separate companies?

Well, SHIT! I didn't think about ANY of that. See! I told you he was a treasure! I was able to look back on my past experience and remind myself that I don't like traveling for business. I love traveling for adventure and with my family, but if I'm traveling for business, I don't really like that. And, again, I don't love managing people. I had to look back on the lessons I learned years before as a sales trainer and manager and be REALLY honest with myself. It sucked, but the clarity I gained from going through the motions on that was invaluable.

The clarity and decision to not move forward with expansion was the easy part. Now I had to do the difficult part. I had to go back to these gentlemen who I respected and admired so much, and I had to thank them for the opportunity. I had to tell them, "Thank you so much for thinking that I would make a good partner. But unfortunately, this is not the direction that I want to go to."

To their credit, both of them were very gracious and they were very understanding. And one even said, "Hey, we just want you to be happy. If you're not happy, no big deal."

I'm pretty sure they went on to find someone else to take advantage of that opportunity, which is great. I'm happy that they did, because it was so hard for me to be honest with myself and say, "This is not the opportunity for me." It was such a great opportunity, but it wasn't a great opportunity for me.

I ran into a similar situation with my own business, not with expanding into other states, but expanding in general. What I thought I wanted was a big company with lots of employees and lots of producers. In the insurance world, commission-only salespeople are called producers.
I thought I wanted to have lots of employees, lots of producers, and lots of business. When I started down that path again, I remembered I don't like to manage salespeople but not soon enough. In the excitement of owning a big

company with lots of employees, I made a decision that wasn't a good one. I expanded our office space. It's a classic example of "Oh, I need more space because I'm going to grow." So, you sign a three-year lease on a space that's way too big and in excess of what you need. Classic example of someone who is NOT clear on where they are and where they want to go.

And then I made the decision to not expand my company. Why? Because I FINALLY learned the lesson. I believe God will teach you a lesson again and again until you FINALLY learn that lesson. So, here I was with all of this space that I didn't need. It was a bad financial decision. What was I going to do? Luckily enough, this was the last time I had to go through that because I absolutely learned that lesson. The good news is the space was divided up in ways that I was able to sublease, and cut some of our losses. I wasn't able to break even, but that's okay. If a lesson isn't physically painful or it doesn't cost me money, I'm not going to learn it. I'm happy to say that is the last time I will learn that lesson, but let's look at the flip side of it.

What if I wasn't comfortable enough admitting that was not really what I wanted to do? What if I continued down that path? What if, even though I knew it was wrong, I still continued to hire commission-only salespeople, knowing that I didn't want to do that and I didn't want to go down that path, knowing that I would become miserable, that I would probably burn out and create a monster inside of my company that I couldn't manage? It would have been terrible. But because I had the courage to stop and say, "This isn't what I want. Yes, I thought it was what I wanted at a certain point, but I've changed my mind" – because I had the courage to say that – the damage was minimal. I was able to learn the lesson and move on again.

That was a couple of years ago. And I promise this time I've learned the lesson. So, if you've made a decision that you're not happy with, don't be scared to turn around and say, "I don't think that's gonna work for me anymore." Don't be scared to say you were wrong. Get clarity on what you want. If there's anything that's in your life that's not fitting, it's okay to release it.

Are you feeling any shame over past decisions and choices that you made? I have definitely been there. Visit www.TheLadyCEObook.com for a special video I posted about **How I handle Shame.**

How many identities do you have?

In our society, our identity has become whatever it is that we do for money. When we meet people, we say, "Hi, what do you do?" With this question, we are asking, "How do you make a living? How do you feed your family? What do you do for money?" Because of that, I feel like our society has become single-identity-focused. Let's look at it in the form of relationships. Two people meet and start dating. They have basically two separate lives, separate jobs, separate interests, separate friends, things that make them into individuals. But then something happens. They start to spend all of their time together. They start hanging out with their friends less and less or the same friends all the time. They stop going out and doing the things that interest them on a regular basis. Guys' night and ladies' night out are things of the past. They start to become consumed with each other. And it's almost as if their separate personalities disappear. Then the individual that attracted them to the relationship in the first place is gone. They become one in the relationship. And then sometimes all they have is this relationship. It's a sad story. But it doesn't have to be this way.

Let's look at it. Career-wise, it's the same story. You become obsessed with working and climbing the corporate ladder, or you start your own business and become obsessed with that. Being a business owner, you have to understand marketing, hiring, firing, building the business in general. I completely understand. When I was twenty-one, I decided to become a full-time realtor. Now, this isn't shocking because I had been a part-time realtor for about six months while I worked at an accounting firm in downtown Kansas City. And after about six months, I decided to take the leap, quit my full-time job and all the security that it offered, and decided to be self-employed full-time. I worked on a team and it was busy, busy, busy from the get-go. Back in the day, when I was a realtor, when a person worked on a team, it was actually the responsibility of the team leader to provide everyone else with leads and business to follow up on. The team leader was essentially "the rainmaker" and the rest of the team benefited from it. That's why you joined a team. That's why you gave up a certain percentage of your commission to the team leader.

The team leader that I worked with was absolutely brilliant with lead generation. He had a proven system and was dedicated to growing the team. So, I was always busy. He was always handing me a steady stream of business. All I had to do was follow up the way he taught me and close the deal, which was good. Until it wasn't. I was so young, hungry, and eager for the money and to be successful that I worked nonstop. While my friends went on float trips, went on ski trips, and took long weekends away on different adventures, all I did was chase the money. Morning, afternoon, evening... All I did was work and think about work. I even worked on the weekends. We worked all weekend long. I did take a few days off here and there, but it was never for long.

One perfect example was when my brother was leaving the army. I had the incredible idea to fly from Kansas City to North Carolina and join him on his road trip home. I was supposed to be gone for five days. The team I worked with was all set to take care of all of my clients. My brother was so excited to finally be home that we only stopped for about seven hours the first night to sleep. We just kept driving so he could get home. It was a great trip full of lots of great food and conversation. Because we got home a few days early, I didn't really know what to do with myself. It was almost uncomfortable not to work. So instead of taking a few extra days to relax or handle personal stuff, I called the team and let them know I was back in town and could jump right back in.

And where did that get me? Definitely not where I thought it would. Several times in my eight-year real-estate career, it got me so burnt out that I tried to leave. But because it had become my one and only identity, I kept getting sucked back in. Several times, I took other jobs or tried to go down other career paths, but I couldn't get past this identity of being a realtor. I couldn't get past the "Well, if I'm not a realtor, then what am I?" It had consumed me. It had become a part of me and I just couldn't let it go. That is until I crashed and burned hard, but we'll save that story for another chapter. I promise it's worth the wait.

But it's not an issue only with professionals. What about parents who become consumed in the mom or dad role? The sports parent? As the kids get older and try to become independent, the parents cling to them because their children have become their only identity. Unfortunately, this leads to parents with an empty house and nothing to talk about once the kids are gone. Most people don't even see it coming. We see it all the time. Stories of couples who have been married for fifteen or twenty years, but then the kids grew up and moved out. The kids had been the center of their universe for so long that without the kids, they had nothing in common. They lost their identity as their children left home to go on with their lives.

There is a different way. I promise. I've worked very hard to have multiple identities. Unlike multiple personalities, multiple identities can be a good thing. Here are just a few of the identities I currently have. I'm a wife of sixteen-plus years. I'm a mom of two incredible sons. I'm a business owner. I'm a leader in my community. I'm a business development coach. I'm a dog mom. I'm a runner. Ok... I think you get the idea. You might be thinking, "Okay, great. But what does that all matter?" The reason it all matters is because one is the loneliest number. Way too many people find their self-worth in just one identity. And it's incredibly dangerous.

I'm happy to report that, at this point, my marriage is pretty rock-solid, but what if that changed? What if my husband came to me one day because he decided being my husband wasn't his identity anymore, that being married to me is no longer part of the identity that he wants? That would be terrible for me. What if he died? That would be even worse, but it wouldn't make me question my identity or question my self-worth because I have other identities that help feed into my self-worth.

One day, my children will grow up and move out of the house. I mean, raising independent human beings that go on to live their own lives is the goal, right? Now, will it be sad when the boys move out? Of course! But we are already making plans for the next chapter in our lives. When we don't have kids to look after anymore, spoiler alert, we're moving to the beach and becoming surfing bums in our fifties and sixties. I'm really looking forward to that identity more than any identity that I have tried on.

There have been a lot of identities that I have tried that fit. And there have been a lot of identities that didn't fit and that's okay. The key here is to just keep trying them on. If you feel like your identity is wrapped up in one single area, I encourage you to change that. It's okay to start slowly and build up to a few. It's okay to leave some behind. As you discover new ones, I give you permission to change your identity. Just make sure that you have more than one.

As great as my life is, I recently became very bored and uninspired with myself. If you are feeling that way also, visit www.TheLadyCEObook.com for a special video I posted titled **I was BORED and UNINSPIRED**.

Are you lying?

I feel like in our society today we have a problem with lying.

No, I'm not saying you are a liar.

No, I'm not saying we lie to other people.

I am saying we lie to OURSELVES. We lie and hide the truth about what we REALLY want in our lives. We hide it away and tuck it so deep down inside that we can't even tell ourselves the truth most of the time. We hide from it like scared little children with a secret that we don't want to share with anyone. We get to the point where we aren't even honest with ourselves about what we really want because it becomes lost.

When I was growing up, I wasn't one of those kids that had big dreams. There was no "When I grow up, I want to be..." I had no idea what I wanted to be. I had no idea where I wanted my life to go. And you know what? That's ok. I don't see that as a bad thing. Growing up, I didn't see a lot of examples of adults living their dreams. Growing up, I didn't know anyone who could honestly proclaim they were living their best lives.

The way I grew up showed me something different. It gave me clarity around what I DIDN'T want and that has been a powerful tool in my life. I remember one year my dad telling his third wife to take my brother and me shopping for school clothes. For most kids, it's not a super-exciting time but it's not terrible because you get new shoes and clothes. That's not exactly how we grew up.

This specific year was right around the eighth grade or so, when most young people really start to become aware of what they look like and the clothes they wear. Instead of going to the mall or department stores like most kids, we went to the Goodwill. Now I'm not saying you can't find some incredible things at the Goodwill. You absolutely can. But for a young person who is hyperaware of what the other kids are wearing and, more importantly, what you are NOT wearing, this is something difficult. For a young person who just wants to fit in and wear new clothes, this can be a difficult time.

That specific year, school shopping had a budget of $20 per child and the only place to stretch that money was at the Goodwill store. It was an incredible example of where I didn't want to be when it was time for me to take my kids school shopping.

At this point, you can probably guess I didn't have many examples of what winning financially looked like. Clearly, when we lived with my dad, it was a mess. We were on welfare and he never kept a job. He bounced around from job to job, which meant we moved a lot because he didn't pay the bills. One of the "lessons" my dad taught me growing up was that you don't sign for a registered letter. Ever.

Because if someone is sending you a registered letter that you need to sign for, it's probably a collection notice from a past pill, and if you don't sign for it, then they can't prove you ever got the letter. Yeah... I know – a real piece of work. Can you imagine even living like that?

I guess a bonus of living on welfare is that you get food stamps. I can honestly say that thanks to food stamps, we had food in the house. We didn't always have electricity because my dad didn't pay the bills, but somehow, we always had water and food. It was nice not to have to worry about those things. I was clean because we had water, and I was fed because we had food. I know it sounds weird, but when I look back on it, I just think, "Well, it could have been worse!"

Being a welfare recipient also came with the added bonus of being on the free-lunch program at school. I remember racing down the hall every Monday in high school at lunch to jump in line to grab my lunch card. That little green paper lunch card came with so many mixed emotions.

I was so grateful to be getting a hot lunch every day. But I also had the uncomfortable feeling that everyone knew I was getting free lunch and I somehow felt ashamed about it. I can look back on that now at the ripe age of forty-two and smile. I smile because the truth is that no one was really paying attention to me. At that point in our lives, all of my peers were worried about what others thought of them. I am sure most of them had the same weird mixed emotions about one or more things in their own lives.

I can't say that living with my mom was any better; it was just different. My mom ALWAYS had a job. As a matter of fact, she worked in a factory in Kansas City for over forty years. She just recently retired from that job. When we lived with my mom, we always had lunch money and school clothes. What we also had was a daily dose of negativity. Lots of negativity.

With my dad's wife, I truly believe she loved him. My dad was a master manipulator and I believe his wife believed the bullshit dreams he sold her on a regular basis. A few years in, she recognized what a huge mistake she'd made by marrying him but it took her a while to get out of the marriage. That's not how things were with my mom and her husband.

I can honestly say I think my mom and her husband hated each other. I know it sounds crazy but I am not even joking. They were together for almost forty years before he died, and I believe they were both miserable every single day of their marriage. I didn't understand it then, and I still don't understand it now. My mom tried to leave a few times but the familiar always pulled her back in and she just couldn't leave.

The twisted part is that I learned two incredible lessons from watching two people be miserably married for forty years. There is a fine line between love and hate, and those two crossed the line from the very start. No, that was not one of the lessons I learned. The first lesson I learned is that life is way too short to be married to someone who doesn't make you happy. John and I have been married for almost seventeen years. Being his wife and partner is a huge part of who I am. But if it doesn't bring me joy or, even worse, it makes me miserable, I shouldn't continue in the marriage. I know that might sound harsh, and I am not trying to give you marriage advice. You gotta do what's best for you.

The second lesson I learned by being around so much negativity and tension on a daily basis is that I can't control the energy of people around me. I've seen this play out differently in other people. Some became the entertainer to try to lift the mood and make everyone happy. Some became the people pleaser to ease the tension that is going on around them. Me? Well, I decided to just worry about my own damn self and to control my own energy. I know this sounds weird but it's how I cope.

The gift I got from all of the negativity is the realization that I cannot change people. I can only lead myself and control myself. And you know what? Usually, that's enough. Because when I stay calm and cool, usually those around me will follow the lead. With my own family now, if I stay positive in all situations and say, "Ok, here's the good thing about this…," it usually brings the stress level down. Another way I know it's working? In situations where I don't keep my cool, it's my husband or my sons saying to me, "Ok, here's the good thing about this…," so my words come shining right back at me.

When was the last time you sat down and wrote down exactly what you want in your life? I used to do it every few years and now I do it at least once a year, sometimes several times a year. I give you PERMISSION to be honest with yourself about what you REALLY want in your life. I give you permission to be honest with yourself about all the circles or buckets or whatever you call them in your life.

Is your income where you want it?

Is your family life where you want it?

Is your marriage where you want it?

Is your fitness level where you want it?

It's ok to not know exactly what you want in each section of your life. Having the courage to be clear on what you DON'T want will start you on a journey to figuring out what you DO want.

Have you ever thought you knew what you wanted but ended up failing? Same here! If you are feeling that way, visit www.TheLadyCEObook.com for a special video I posted titled **Why are we so scared to fail?**

Is it a goal or a standard?

How old were you when you started to become aware of goals and goal planning?

I knew when I was fifteen that I wanted "more" for my life.

I knew I wanted to be "something" when I grew up. Of course, I had no idea what the something was but I knew I wanted to be something.

I knew I wanted to go to college when I graduated from high school, but only because I thought college was what "successful" people did. I didn't understand that college was actually only one of many wonderful options ahead of me.

It wasn't until I was in my early twenties that I really started to understand goal setting. Of course, I understood the whole

"New Year's resolution" thing.
I understood WANTING to do a better job and have a better life, but I didn't understand how to be specific or to actually set goals. Tell me it's the same for you just to make me feel better. Lie to me if you have to.

I began to understand the power of writing goals down after my divorce. Yep, remember a few chapters back when we talked about not marrying a bad decision? Yep, it was right after that when I started to truly understand the power of setting goals. I was still in my early twenties, and I knew I would get married again and, of course, have kids someday. But I also knew it would be different the second time. I knew it would be VERY different the second time. I knew I had to be clear and specific on exactly what and who I wanted in my life as my next partner.

I sat myself down one day and made a list. I wrote out all the qualities I wanted in a future partner and it was glorious. I had the courage to be honest with myself about what I wanted and who I wanted to be with. I was honest about what I needed and what I admired in a partner. I was honest about who I needed the man to be so that I would respect and honor him.

And then came the SUPER-hard part... I had to take it one step further and ask myself, "Now what kind of a woman would that man want to be with?" Oh, boy, that was hard to do. I had to look at my life and myself and get clear on the parts that needed to be cleaned up. I'm not gonna lie... ALL the parts needed to be cleaned up. I got to work over the next few years and was able to get all the areas of my life in order.

I would love to sit here and tell you that John magically appeared off the pages of my "wants" list but that's not exactly how it happened. I probably should have stopped dating while I was working on me but that's not fun so... It took a few tries, but I did finally get it right. I mean... obviously because you know I've been married for almost seventeen years. It's ok. You can call me Captain Obvious. It won't hurt my feelings.

As magical as that experience was, it still took years for me to get to a point of setting goals every single year. And I'm not talking about wishy-washy stuff like New Year's Eve resolutions. I am talking about written-down goals with action steps attached to each one. I'm talking about actual real-life plans to make my life better.

I have been able to accomplish so many incredible things in my life because I had the courage to write them down and then lay a path out to get them accomplished. Sure, there have been lots of big goals that seemed like stretch goals. Goals so big that I had no idea how on earth I was going to accomplish them. Goals so big that I almost laughed as I wrote them. Almost... and then I ended up laughing all the way across the goals finish line.

A common theme in my life is "Well... I didn't see that coming." I mean that in both incredible and not so incredible ways. I knew that I would accomplish a lot and have a great life if I continued to set goals. What I didn't see coming was that, as I accomplished each goal, my standards would increase. It's the funniest thing. As I accomplish goals and see what I am capable of, I accept less mediocrity from my life and from those around me.

We set financial goals. As we hit these goals, it became unacceptable and uncomfortable for us to have less than a certain amount of reserves or money invested in our accounts. We basically reset and raise the goal.

We set goals for our business. As we hit those goals, it became unacceptable and uncomfortable to have members on our team that didn't have the same goals and standards that we had. I've had to up-level my office team several times. I am proud to say that I have the best team I have ever had. But there were times when our team was not the best. We didn't have standards around performance and prior experience, and it showed. As we decided to become better business owners and leaders, we closed these gaps and made hiring better team members a priority.

We set fitness goals in our family. Now, let's be real about this one. I had set plenty of fitness goals before. There had been plenty of times when my eating had been on point, but I wasn't moving my body. There had been plenty of times when I was moving my body, but my eating was not on point. I have been a pretty avid runner for several years. I speak from experience when I say you can't outrun a bad diet. Believe me because I tried!

Finally, in early 2020, I decided to change all of that. I decided not to just set goals, but to up my standards for how I treated my body. Honestly, I just got tired of my own weak-ass excuses and bullshit. I just got tired of me. I changed the way I ate. I got outside every day for a walk or a run, and I started lifting weights consistently.

Not only did I start to change my body, but the bodies around me started changing. I know that sounds insane but it's true! My behaviors at home changed and John and the boys started to notice. They started catching on and started wanting to change their bodies also. I ended up slimming down quite a bit but so did John and the boys.

It didn't stop with my family. Several friends and people on the socials noticed and started asking me questions. I was open about my journey and was happy to share everything with them. Because of that, several of them got tired of their own excuses and they took control of their bodies. It's been such an incredible thing to be a part of.

I set goals in relation to the types of people I would spend time with. I've never really let a lot of people into my circle out of default, but at some point, I had to set some parameters. As I consciously up-leveled my circle, my life started to get better. My goals started to get bigger. I started to see more in myself and expect more of myself. My standards increased for those around me.

At this point, I have some of the winningest friends ever! So many people in my life are winning at high levels. They are winning in business, in their family, and in their physical lives. They are leading others and helping others up-level along the way. Of course, it's not all sunshine and rainbows for me or my circle. But we look at things differently. When we fail (and we DO!) there's no "Oh, don't worry, Jess, because you TRIED YOUR HARDEST..." Nope. There's no patting each other on the back because we "tried." Trying your hardest is for your kids; it's not for you. In the face of failure, my circle asks two questions:

1. Did you REALLY want that goal to begin with?
2. If you DID really want that goal, what lesson did you learn that will help you when you go for that goal again?

It's only recently that I started to see myself as an encourager and a leader that could offer help and guidance to others. It's because my circle saw more in me than I could ever see in myself. I suggest you get a circle like that.

If you feel like some of your Standards are starting to slip, visit www.TheLadyCEObook.com for a special video I posted about **The lesson my dogs taught me about standards**. It's about setting standards and then holding the line!

Are you lonely or just alone?

When was the last time you did something all by yourself?

No, I mean it. When was the last time you went to a new restaurant by yourself?

When was the last time you went shopping by yourself?

When was the last time you took yourself on a date?

Too many times we wait for other people to go with us before we'll go and do what we want to do.

You want to try a new restaurant, but your friends don't go with you. So you end up never going.

You want to go see a movie, but your spouse or partner doesn't want to see it. So, you don't go.

A couple of years ago, I had the incredible opportunity to go to New York City. The reason I was going to New York City was because I was invited to Elton John's annual New York City Gala fundraiser. That's right. THE Elton John! He does two big fundraisers every year for his charities. One is in Los Angeles and the other is in New York City. I was in the amazing position to get a seat at a table at the New York City one with the option of getting a few more seats if I wanted to bring anyone along.

A few months before the event, I told my husband about it. I was so excited.

"We're going to go to New York City! We're going to see the sights! We're going to get all dressed up! And we're going to go to a big fancy party!"

Needless to say, my husband was not interested. He wanted nothing to do with it. He loves New York City. He loves food and seeing the sights. But what he doesn't love is putting on a tuxedo and going to fancy parties. He also doesn't love leaving his little man cubs at home. He was a hard "No, thank you" on the fancy trip to New York.

One of the things I adore most about my husband is he encourages me to do things that I want to do. Sure, he will bite the bullet on a regular basis and go do things with me that he doesn't want to. But if he really doesn't want to go, he still encourages me to go and do it on my own. He encourages me to keep my individuality.

So, we decided I was going to go to New York City without him. He said, "Go and have a wonderful time. Enjoy the city. Eat all the food. Take pictures. FaceTime me if you see any celebrities. I can't wait to hear all about it when you get home."

If I'm being completely honest, I really didn't want to go to New York City all by myself. It's not that I am uncomfortable being all by myself. It's just that this was an incredible opportunity for adventure, and I knew I could offer the opportunity to other people. So, I reached out to several of my friends and invited them along. I gave them all the details, including the cost. Several said they really wanted to go but had to fine-tune a few things to see if they could make it official.

In the end, for one reason or another, no one ended up being able to go. It looked like I was going to end up going to New York City all by myself. But I was willing to go by myself. I didn't second guess and say, "Well, if so and so can go, then I will go." Nope. I was down for this adventure even if no one showed up and wanted to go with me. And in the end, no one showed up and it looked like I was going alone.

So that's what I did. I packed a bag and headed off to New York City! And I gotta tell ya... I am SO glad I did!

I found a fabulous hotel in the Garment District. The hotel room was super tiny, but it was super fancy, and I loved it. The king-size bed took up at least three-quarters of the room and it was so cozy and fluffy. After I checked into my room, I realized I was only a short walk from Times Square. I packed a bottle of water and a map and headed off for adventure!

I wandered around for a couple of hours, stopping occasionally just to look around and watch the people go by. After that, I treated myself to lunch. I stopped in at a small burger place and sat at the counter by myself. I ordered a massive bacon cheeseburger with all the ridiculous toppings. After that, I headed back to my room to relax for the rest of the evening. I don't remember what I had for dinner. I'm sure it was just room service. When I travel by myself, I don't tend to go out at night alone. You might think I am crazy for traveling by myself, but I promise I try to stay safe.

The next morning, I met up with a small group of people for an incredible training. That training was part of the reason I was in New York. It was a private event for everyone in the group that was going to the Elton John fundraiser. We spent several hours together in this super-cool loft meeting area. It actually had a phone booth in the meeting area. Yes, I climbed in and had someone take my picture. I mean… of course! After an incredible lunch that was catered in, it was back to my hotel room to get ready for the party.

I feel like most women are thinking right about now, "What did you wear?" and that's one of the BEST parts of the whole story. I got to wear a floor-length sequin gown that looked like something out of the movies. I am not even joking. I could have walked straight out of the *Frozen* movie in this beautiful dress. It was the most beautiful ice-baby-blue dress and it fit like a dream. It had a perfect V-neckline that was elegant and comfortable but didn't show too much cleavage. I'm just not into showing my boobs.

It was the first time I'd ever worn a full-length sequin gown. Unfortunately, it was also the last time I wore a full-length sequin gown. I haven't been to a fancy party since then. But that's an excuse. I guess I should probably put it on and wear it around the house every once in a while.

That would be fun. I should put it on the next time I do the dishes just for the hell of it.

Anyway, back to the story. So, I got dressed up in my super-fancy dress and went down to the hotel lobby. I had made a friend at the front desk the day before. When it's appropriate, I make sure I tip service providers very well. The main reason is that they deserve it, but the secondary reason is that I know I can be a little extra sometimes. On this occasion, that came in the form of: "Hey, would you mind PLEASE taking a few pictures of me in front of the hotel in my super-fancy dress?" Then I jumped in my Uber and went off to the gala.

I'm not sure what I was expecting but I wasn't expecting what I experienced. It was the most incredible event I have ever been to in my entire life. The location was an architectural masterpiece called Cipriani 42nd Street. The building had massive soaring columns out front. The front was lit up with red and purple lights.

It was truly a sight to see on a foggy winter night.

When we pulled up to the event, the valet opened my door. Then he asked me the silliest question ever. He said, "Would you like to enter through the side entrance, or would you like to go in the main entrance and walk the red carpet?" I guess it's a perfectly logical question. I guess some people attending these fancy galas prefer to slip in unnoticed and blend in. But... Um, hello... I'm a girl from Kansas wearing a full-length sequin ice-blue gown! Of course, I'm going to walk the red carpet! It was so fun and entertaining. I stepped on the carpet and the cameras started flashing. No one knew who I was, and I didn't even care. I walked so slowly across that dang red carpet. You would have thought I was walking in wet cement. I was flashing big smiles all the way until I got inside. I'm not sure I will ever get to walk a red carpet again, so you know I was trying to make the most of it.

Of course, the inside was decorated in the most gorgeous and elegant way ever imagined. Let's not even start on the food. Okay. Let's do talk about the food. The whole meal was absolutely incredible, but the one thing I remember most was the very first pasta dish. It was pasta with cheese sauce and cheese crust on top and it was the most incredible pasta I'd ever eaten. Of course, I had to take a picture and send it to John and tell him about this amazing pasta that he was missing out on. There were several celebrities that I recognized at the charity event, and it was the most incredible venue and decorations I'd ever seen in the history of my forty-two-year-old life.

Needless to say, I stayed out way past my bedtime, which is ten o'clock. So, when I stayed out until almost midnight in New York City, it was long after I usually go to bed. I went back to the hotel, called John and told him all about a conversation I had with women's tennis legend Billie Jean King and then fell asleep.

I was flying out the next afternoon, but I had one more stop to make before I headed to the airport. No trip to New York

City is complete without a trip to Tiffany's on 5th Avenue! And, boy, was it a trip to Tiffany's! I live in Kansas City and we have a Tiffany's in a shopping district called The Plaza, but the Tiffany's in Kansas City is a jewelry store. The Tiffany's in New York City is a destination. There are four or five floors at the Tiffany's in New York City, along with a magical cafe. I'm not sure exactly how many stories because I was too mesmerized to count. I just know I walked in and I felt amazing. They have all of the fancy jewelry on the first level and it's bright and very sparkly. But I wasn't looking for jewelry. Not on this trip, anyway.

I was more looking for housewares and other gift-type items. I got to travel up several floors and explore as I went along. I bought all kinds of gifts for myself including my favorite china coffee cup and some new notebooks. I'm a sucker for notebooks, especially ones bound in the beautiful Tiffany Blue canvas.

My visit was in mid-November, so everything was already decorated for

Christmas. One of the Christmas decorations in the store was a massive and gorgeous robot. I know it might sound a little weird that Tiffany's had a robot on display, but it was pretty fantastic. So, there I was with my massive Tiffany's shopping bags – because everything at Tiffany's comes in a beautiful, sometimes oversized, box – standing next to a giant robot. What are the chances? Of course, I asked the nice sales lady to take my picture. I mean, of course, I did!

After that, I headed to the airport, jumped on a plane and flew home. That was it. That was my super-special, two-day trip to New York City all by myself. I get so excited when the pictures show up in my Facebook memory feed. I love looking at the pictures of Tiffany's and the dress I wore and the hotel I stayed in. I love telling my husband, "Oh, I wish you could have had that pasta. It was the most incredible pasta I have ever had."

Had I not gone, I would have missed out on an incredible opportunity. I can honestly say it was a once-in-a-lifetime opportunity. We miss out on way too many things because we wait for other people to come along with us on our journey.

There are things we want to do.

There are experiences we want to have.

There are things we want to go investigate, but we are so worried about not being alone, that we don't go unless other people come with us.

There are times on your journey when you will have to travel alone. I'm not saying you'll be lonely. You'll have your friends; you'll have your family; you'll have your spouse or significant other – just not right by your side.

There are times when you really want to do something or try something, and you will have to go alone. I'm not saying you'll be lonely, but you will physically be alone.

Unfortunately, I think most people are uncomfortable doing things by themselves. I know it can be scary and making memories can definitely be more fun with other people. I just want you to remember that everyone is on their own journey. The things that you want to experience are a part of your journey, but they might not be a part of your friends' or family's journey.

If you keep waiting for others, you will miss out.

Stop waiting.

I love when people tell me they are "too busy with work" to go on adventures or to create memories. If you are feeling like that, visit www.TheLadyCEObook.com and watch a video called **I will never tell you that you work too much.**

Are you an idea generator or an idea killer?

We all have those friends who ALWAYS have new ideas or things they want to try. Every time you turn around, they are saying, "I've got a great idea!"

And you think to yourself, "Oh no, not again! Jesus take the wheel because here's ANOTHER idea." Those people are always coming up with some kind of crazy thing that you just know is never going to work.

On the other side of that coin is the friend that never wants to try anything new. They always do the same things, watch the same shows, eat the same foods, take the same trips, visit the same vacation spots... They live in a bubble and don't want to come out of it. They like things the way they are and feel like nothing ever needs to change.

I've been in both camps in my life. As a default, I am the friend who always has the crazy ideas. I am the friend that has the crazy, big goals. I am the friend that has suggestions for everything and usually can't stop talking about the next adventure. I'm the one that wants to pull people out of their comfort zones and show them how to really live their lives. I'm the friend that believes that there is more to life than just a career and that we need to explore and go see the world.

I believe we all have something called an "idea valve." I know that sounds crazy but just stick with me for a few minutes. I believe good… great… EXCEPTIONAL ideas come to all of us through what I'll call an idea valve. What else can we call it? You know what I mean. The feeling when you have THE BEST idea ever and you have no idea where it came from. That's exactly what I mean by idea valve.

One of my favorite messages to get from my friends is "Hey, I need to chat because I have an idea, I want to run by you." It's not any kind of a pitch or "investment opportunity"; it's never anything like that. It usually doesn't even have anything to do with me. They just have an idea, and they need to talk it out with someone. They need to get an unbiased opinion on whether it's going to work or not. They need someone to tell them the truth and to point out the blind spots they can't see. In my circle, I have a reputation for being that person. It's pretty incredible when I get those messages and jump on those calls.

Most of the ideas I hear are not the best ideas. Let's be real; most ideas are terrible. That's right; I said it! For every three great ideas I have, I have at least seven that ended up being total trash. But that's not the point of the idea valve, in my opinion. The aim is to let the ideas FLOW and go through the valve. A perfect example is a text I got from a dear friend recently. She said, "Call me when you get a minute. I have an idea to run by you. No rush." *Oh, goodie!* I love messages like that.

I called my friend later in the afternoon and we chatted about her idea. It was good. Just good, but the direction of her idea and what she was trying to create was fabulous! After she told me her idea, I asked a few questions so I could understand exactly what she was trying to accomplish with the idea. I made a few suggestions and helped her clarify a few things. By the end of the conversation, we had basically taken the original idea and twisted about 50% of it around to come up with something that was way better.

I thought about the idea for another day or so and then called my friend back with a few more suggestions on how she could move it forward and make it even more incredible. I would have never had this idea on my own, so it was fun to help her with ideas on how to bring it to life. Within a few days, she had ironed out the final details and I saw a post on the socials about the idea we discussed.

That's not always how things happen, of course. There are times when I hear an idea that is so good, I don't have anything to add.

Or times when I don't see the idea working out no matter how we spin it.

Or times when the exact same previous conversation happens but the person who had the idea never ends up doing anything with it. That the saddest part. I hate seeing ideas go to the idea graveyard but that's what happens most of the time.

Every day, people have incredible and life-changing ideas, but they never tell anyone about them. I completely understand that. Most people fall in the category of idea killers and they will squish your idea. It might just be because they are small-minded and can't see the possibility. Or it might be that they actually see the idea for the brilliance it is but they are jealous that you had such a great idea. Whatever the reason, they are negative towards your idea, which causes you to pull back.

When you share something as personal as an idea and it gets a negative review, it can sting. I get that, and that's why I am very careful about who I share my ideas with. I don't just go around spouting off about my ideas to anyone. First, I write them in a book. Then I sit with them and think about them for a while. If I know it's a great idea, I might not "run it by" anyone. The first time anyone hears about it might be when I am announcing it or launching it.

If I do find myself needing input on an idea or feel stuck on a project, there are only a few people I reach out to. The first person I run my ideas by is my husband. He knows me and how my mind works better than anyone. He's also seen me fail my way to success on a regular basis so he knows I can take honest feedback. From there, I have a few close friends that are the next stop. After that, it's up to me to make the final decision on the idea based on the feedback.

Several years ago, I had what I thought was a great idea. I mean, we think ALL of our ideas are great to begin with, right? I don't even remember what the idea was, but for whatever reason, I was asking a lot of people their opinion. I must not have had the confidence to pull the trigger yet. That happens to me sometimes. One day, John asked me why I was getting so many opinions on this one idea. It was a great question because I didn't realize I was questioning the idea so much. What he told me next would forever change the way I processed ideas. He said, "When you really believe in something, you don't ask for a lot of opinions about it. You just make it happen." Wow! He was absolutely right! What he taught me in that moment was that I knew what a great idea was and what one wasn't. I usually knew what needed to happen, and I didn't need a ton of input on the overall idea. I kinda hit the love lottery when I found him, am I right?

Let's go back to my friend who had the good idea and wanted my input. Let's say she never asked my opinion about the idea. She would have maybe launched the good product, but it wouldn't have been fabulous. Because it wasn't fabulous, it might have fizzled and died on the vine. But because she had the courage to open up and ask for my opinion, together, we made the idea even better.

Napoleon Hill talks about the power of the "mastermind" in his classic books. He talks about the concept of when two or more people come together and discuss something, a third separate energy or opinion is actually formed. When my friend and I had the conversation about her idea, we fed off each other's ideas and energy. She would make a suggestion, and then I would build off it and then send it back to her, almost like a game of tennis or something. The ideas and the flow built in a way that would have never happened if we hadn't worked on the idea together.

When you don't give your ideas space to grow or share them with qualified people, the idea valve gets backed up. It starts to shut down and the ideas stop coming. Even a "bad" idea might be worth at least talking through with someone because you never know when that idea will lead to another one.

Give yourself permission to have terrible ideas and, I promise you, great ideas will start to come.

Have you ever been in a downward spiral that you just couldn't get out of? Maybe you are in that right now. If that's you, visit www.TheLadyCEOBook.com and watch the video titled **Stopping a downward spiral**.

I give you permission to quit.

Can you even believe I just said you can quit? I think quitting gets a bad rap. Yes, I know I am going to get some hate mail over that statement. And that's ok with me.

I love all of these quotes and motivational things that talk about "winners never quit" and all that other feel-good jazz. I don't believe it's true. I know plenty of people who dug really deep holes for themselves because of a "never quit" mindset or attitude. People don't want to talk about those stories because they don't feel good.

I found myself in that exact situation many years ago. I couldn't let go of something. I couldn't walk away from something, and it almost ruined my family.

When I was in my early twenties, I decided a career in real estate would be a great idea. I mean, why not! I had been through the process when buying a small home and it didn't seem all that difficult. I had a good corporate job working in the accounting department of a large trucking company. I knew I didn't want to be there forever, so I was keeping my eyes open for opportunities.

Working for that trucking company feels like a lifetime ago. I guess because it was over twenty years ago. It was a nice place to work, but it definitely had a "glass ceiling" when it came to the women in the office. All of the directors and heads of projects were men. I saw the expense reports that came in from the executives every month and some of the charges would not have been female-friendly. I didn't judge or say anything. It wasn't my company, and it wasn't my place to decide if charges got approved or not. The guy that owned the company was Mr. Jones.

No, that is not made up. No, I am not changing the names to protect peoples' identities. That was really his name.

I'll never forget the day one of the ladies said to me, "If you are here long enough, maybe, one day, you will get to be Mr. Jones' secretary!" Wow. The goals and ambition of the women in the office were to be secretaries. I'm not saying that's a bad thing. I'll admit I was pretty young and naïve at that point in my life. I just knew that was not a path I wanted to be on.

As I typed that, I realized this is another perfect example of me not knowing what I wanted in my life but being very clear on what I didn't want in my life.

Being a realtor was an incredible career. Until it wasn't. I was amazing at it. Until I wasn't. It was the best career ever. Until it wasn't. I already started this story a few chapters back in the "identity" chapter. But now, I'm going to tell you how the story ends. Spoiler alert – it EVENTUALLY has a happy ending, but it was difficult to get there.

As I mentioned before, being a realtor had become my identity. At such a young age, it had become my *only* identity. Back in the early 2000s, the market was good. The market had been good for quite some time. I had never had to navigate a down real-estate market like so many other professionals had to. In the blink of an eye, everything started to change in 2008. I won't go into specifics about how the market crashed or how the real-estate bubble burst. There are plenty of articles and movies on all of that. I'm just going to explain how it felt on my end of it all.

In a regular market, a realtor has at least an 80% chance of selling a home that goes on the market. That means, assuming the home is in decent shape and priced right, the realtor has an 80% chance of getting the home sold and collecting the commission check they work so hard to earn. But that's not how things happened, starting in 2008. The downturn of the market meant that the 80% shifted to about 25%. Yep. That meant that all things considered, only about 25% of the homes that came on the market actually ended up selling. What a change.

Unfortunately, something else that started to change that year was me. I was really starting to feel burnt out. I had served for so long that my little heart was all served out. One day, I was sitting on the steps in our house. I was crying. John came and sat by me to try to make me feel better. Being the awesome husband he is, of course, he asked, "What's wrong?" I've told this story several times and, as sad as it is, it's still pretty funny.

"I hate my job! Every time I think about real estate, my clients, or the new leads coming in, I feel sick to my stomach!"

That's super sad, right? Well, the funny part is that we had no idea that I was pregnant with our first son. The sick to my stomach and nausea that I felt was morning sickness! But in my mind, I had associated all of that with not wanting to be in real estate anymore.

As with most situations, things got worse before they got better. Over the next two years, we were blessed with two incredible sons. I think people take for granted the miracle of healthy babies, but we sure didn't. These little guys became our lives. Our boys were born fourteen months apart, and we considered ourselves lucky.

Unfortunately, the background of my life was a complete tornado. I wasn't happy being in real estate. I was worn out from being pregnant for so long. I was worn down from the sleepless night. In the end, my income plummeted, and John just held the pieces together the best he could. As much as I wanted to leave real estate, where was I going to go? I was pregnant and didn't feel like I had any options. Because it had become my identity, I couldn't let it go. Emotionally and physically, I was a complete wreck.

Obviously, hindsight is 20/20. I can look back on it now and see that it was just time for me to explore more things in my career. I can give myself the grace that I refused to give myself then. I can see that after eight years in real estate, I was ready for something else. When someone leaves a profession or career to explore something new, it's not a bad thing. But for some reason, I couldn't see it like that.

I had two high-risk pregnancies that took their toll on me. I had postpartum depression, which moms don't like to talk about. I had all the crazy hormones and emotions that come with being pregnant and giving birth. Any one single life event that we went through during that time would have been hard for someone to handle. But we handled three major life events in the span of about twenty-four months. We coped until we couldn't. One day, it all came to a stop.

It was my birthday, and John took me to lunch. I was eating chicken wings when he dropped the hammer on me. "You have to get a job."

"Wait, what? I have a job."

But apparently this part-time playing in real estate that I had been doing over the last two years was not enough to keep us on track financially. We had done well for many years, so we had savings tucked away. Now my beloved husband and partner had to tell me that it was running out. We had made financial decisions like buying our home based on a household income of a certain amount. And I wasn't keeping up my end of the agreement.

I was crushed.

I was devastated.

I was heartbroken.

At first, I was really upset. This identity that I had held so tightly for so long was no longer serving me or my family. Even worse, it was starting to drag us down and pull us backwards. As difficult as it was for me to accept this, it was so freeing. In the moment, it felt like the worst thing that could have happened, but it wasn't. It was actually the best thing.

I'm happy to say that things started to change that very day. Why? Because I was ready. This conversation with my husband was the push I needed to finally let go and move on. That very day, I created a resume and started thinking about what I wanted in my next career. Being that I had been self-employed for so long, I couldn't be too picky about what my next move was. I knew that the name of the game was to just get back in the workforce to get the money flowing and then figure it out from there.

It took about two months before I had a new position in life. It was at a call center for a large company. While the work was slightly soul sucking, they offered a safe, warm place to work, plus great medical benefits and tuition reimbursement. I was happy to take advantage of all of that. These perks ended up setting me up for my next position.

It took me over ten years to finally finish my bachelor's degree. I hear some people can do it in four years, but that wasn't me. I took the long, drawn-out route. Had I not swallowed my pride and decided to do what was best for my family, I might not have finished my degree. Let alone have a company pay for the tuition and books. It was a pretty sweet deal. After a few years,

I found myself in a pharmaceutical sales role that I excelled at.

From where I stand now, I can see it was such a great move for me to finally release the identity of working in real estate. There is a statistic somewhere that says people change careers at least four times in their lives. So why did I have such a hard time with it? The super-sad part about this story is that I labeled myself as a failure for several years after leaving real estate. No one else saw me as that but I had given myself the label. It's the perfect example of how we are so hard on ourselves. The story I told myself was that I failed out of real estate. It breaks my heart to think of that now. I didn't fail. Things changed and I stopped trying. By making a career switch, I was looking out for my family and setting myself up for a much brighter future.

So many times, what we personally see as quitting is actually PIVOTING! We aren't quitting; we are making a decision to change directions in our lives. We are making a decision to start moving away from one thing to start moving in the direction of something better. The real problems come when people don't or won't allow themselves to pivot.

If you look around your life and you know you need to make big changes in certain areas, please just have the courage to do it. Don't hang on to something too long that no longer serves you. By releasing it, you are making room in your life for something better to come in and change everything for you.

I get asked all the time "Jessica, when does it get easier?" Go to www.TheLadyCEOBook.com and watch the video titled **When does it get easier** for my thoughts on that.

Are you prepared for the burnout that's coming?

Is that a weird question? Most people talk about how to AVOID burnout but not me. I am going to suggest you lean into it. I want to talk about how to EXPECT it and how to deal with it when it finally does show up.

As I have already openly shared, I have faced burnout many times before. And guess what? I know it's coming again. I have been blessed with an "all or nothing" type of mentality when it comes to building things. I go ALL-IN for long periods of time until I just can't go all-in anymore. The problem previously was that there was no ending to my all-in. There was no slow-down season or exit strategy. I was going all-in indefinitely with no end in sight. That was a problem.

Do you ever get to the point where you are ready to just give in? Where you just don't want to be an adult anymore? Where you look around and one of two things has happened. Either you have given it your all and it's still not enough, or you have given it your all, it has gone REALLY well, and now you have built your own prison. If the answer is yes, then good. That means I am not alone.

If the answer is no, then you have never played full-out.

Most of the people I am lucky enough to associate with serve at a very high level. I think that makes the burnout even worse. We serve and serve and serve the best we can until we just can't serve any more. Most of us in the service industry tend to put everyone else first. The company comes first. The clients come first. The needs of others always seem to come before our needs. By always putting others first, we also take on their stress and their needs, and we have no time or energy to process our own wants and needs.

I found myself in this exact situation a few years ago. It wasn't too long after I started my insurance business. I am good at lots of things, but my true gift is connecting with people. As I was building my insurance business, I spent a good amount of time connecting with people I knew I could serve at a high level. Luckily for me, that means that I received a lot of insurance referrals. When I say a lot, I mean over 300 in my first year in insurance. As incredible as that sounds, I received over 600 in my second year. That sounds great, right? Well... it was for the most part. Except when it wasn't.

One day, I looked up and realized I had basically built my own prison. I had built that thing one relationship, one referral, one brick at a time. I wasn't really surprised because I knew it would eventually happen. It was frustrating to be in the middle of it, but I had actually anticipated it happening. The first way I deal with burnout is I actually expect it. I mentioned it to a few of my friends and, of course, they had experienced the same thing. The sad part was that some of them couldn't see past it and they couldn't get out of it.

With my insurance business, I knew what my next step was going to be. Because I had built an incredible system that was bringing in new business, I had to start looking at what I was doing and start delegating things. I think where most business owners get tripped up is they see that they need help but they are so stuck in working *in* their business that they never take the time to work *on* their business. It can be tough when you have a certain way of doing things and you are scared to trust other people to do certain things. They can mess up. Yes, they can. Sometimes, they actually mess up big. It happens but it will still be ok.

There is an incredible gift in burnout if it's the type that had you working full-out because you have built something that needs you. If you have the type of burnout that comes from going all-in and nothing is happening, then go back and reread the chapter on quitting because you might have a decision to make. When you have burnout because there is so much work to be done, that's a good thing. No, really, I promise it is. It means you are building something and can start to step away from certain things and lean into other things. I saw the burnout was coming. When I built my own prison, it meant that I had enough new business coming in that I could start hiring new team members to carry some of the load. I knew I would need a team to handle what I was creating, and I was able to pick them one person at a time.

Let's all just take a moment to acknowledge that hiring and training new people can absolutely be a drag. Anyone who has built anything involving team members will tell you that. It can add to the bog down and it can add to the burnout and stress. It's just a part of the process. The super-fun part is when you have them all trained and ready to go and they quit, or you have to fire them. Again, it's all part of the process. And we expect it and anticipate it; we know how to deal with it. It's like when you take a trip on an airplane. What do they spend time talking about before you even leave the ground? "In the event of a crash..." That's right! Before the trip even starts, they are talking about what's going to happen when or if the plane crashes. They don't try to hide from it or pretend it's not potentially going to happen. They get it out in the open and talk about it. I want you to see burnout the same way.

Another way I help get myself through burnout is by remembering what I am fighting for. Burnout should only be a season. Something we go through, not get stuck in. So, when it hits, I remind myself why I started in the first place. I keep the reason why I started front and center, so I remember what the end goal is.

Let's be honest. I am not changing the world by owning an insurance company in the middle of the United States. But I am changing someone's world with what I do. I have incredible referral partners that know they can count on me and my team to take care of their clients once they pull us into the transactions. We have clients in our agency that know we are honest and do our best to make sure the unimaginable is covered in their policies. They can trust us to not cut corners or give them bare minimums or state minimum coverages. I have a team of three that know they have a safe, warm place to come to work every day. They don't worry about getting a paycheck or worry about not feeling supported or heard in our office. They know John and I will do our best to take care of them.

Again, I might not be changing the world, but I am changing someone's world and that's enough for me.

I haven't always been clear on my WHY. That's something that has become clear over the last few years. For me, it was always a feeling that I couldn't quite put into words. Over the last few years, I've come to realize that the word I have been looking for is FREEDOM. That's my why.

Freedom to do what I want with my time. My parents never came to school functions or had much time for me and my brother. I want to do all the mom stuff with my boys.

Freedom to go on dates with my husband whenever I want. My marriage is important to me and I want to put lots of time into it. Plus, I still really like spending time with John and look forward to it. We have lunch together several times a week.

Freedom to buy what I want when I want. Remember that story about the school shopping at the Goodwill? If I see an incredible pair of pink Nike running shoes online, I want the freedom to buy them without having to go check my budget.

Freedom to live my life on my terms. Whatever I decide those terms are.

You need to be clear on why you started. Don't give me some made-up answer that sounds good to everyone else. I am not asking you to share it with anyone else. I am asking you to be honest with yourself. I love when people tell me they are "doing this for my family" but they never spend time with their family. They cry from the rooftops that they are stressed because they want to provide for their family and they never even invest in those relationships. I also love when people tell me they are "doing this for my financial future" but they have no idea what their profits are each month or what their balance sheets are.

Those kinds of silly answers will NOT get you through when complete burnout sets in. You better get straight on why you are working your tail off. It has to be what's really important to YOU because there will be plenty of times when YOU are alone.

Need help getting through burn out? It can be a struggle. If you are going through any kind of difficult situation, visit www.TheLadyCEOBook.com and watch the video titled **How I attack every situation**.

Do you REALLY want it or does it just sound good to want it?

As I've mentioned before, I have been pretty serious about my goal planning for a few years now. I really started getting serious about five years ago. I actually started planning annual goal-setting trips for myself. For the first few years, I went to Florida for a few days. I found a hotel right on the beach. I would spend several hours a day sitting by the ocean, dreaming about where I wanted my life to go. It was a pretty magical experience.

Three years ago, I started staying local. I do a lot of traveling during the year and I didn't want to add another trip to my agenda in December. I know some people who start planning their next year much earlier, but I am not usually ready until mid to late December. I like to squeeze every drop out of each calendar year before I move on to the next one.

There's an old historic hotel with an incredible spa about an hour from my house. I head there for a few days to map out the next year of my business, my personal goals, and our family goals. Of course, I ask the family's opinion on our goals because their goals are just as important to me as mine are. Then I lock myself away and create the magic.

My goal planning is a four-step process. The hotel is where I do steps two, three, and four. It's a very simple process because I am a simple person, but I take it very seriously. By the time I am done, I feel like I have created magic. A few years back, I noticed that I was writing things down just to write things down. Almost as if I was throwing everything against the wall to see what would actually stick. If I thought it sounded good as a goal in the next year, I would write it on the list. It's almost as if I felt pressure to write down lots of things, I wanted to accomplish just so I could check things off as I got them done.

Do you ever find yourself needing to feel like you have accomplished things? Even if those things aren't really a challenge? There's just something so satisfying about writing something down and then checking it off as if you really did something special. But some of my goals didn't feel special. And they sure didn't feel like much of a challenge. It's almost as if my goals started to become a little boring and predictable.

I have this crazy theory. I think if we can actually see how the goal is going to be accomplished, then it's not big enough. A little crazy, right? Aren't you supposed to be able to map out your goals? Aren't you supposed to be able to see the finish line and actually achieve the goal? If you can map it out and easily achieve it, then I feel like you are selling yourself short.

Let's walk through a financial goal as an example. Let's say you want to save $10,000 in one year. You have done the math and you know that comes out to $833.34 per month. You have done your budget and looked at all of your expenses. You know for sure that you can get to the magic number of $833.34 each and every month. Boom! Goal set and goal achieved.

But... what if you actually pushed yourself and set the yearly goal at $15,000? Oh, that's a little scarier, right? Now, that's actually going to make you uncomfortable. That's going to require you to get creative and really push yourself. In my opinion, the $10,000 goal isn't big enough. Let's say you FAIL at the $15,000 goal. Let's say you fail so miserably that you only end up with $13,932 at the end of the year. Did you really fail? I don't think so. You might not have accomplished the actual goal, but by pushing yourself, you went so much further than if you had settled on the original goal.

As I have mentioned, I am a runner. Previously, my running has been very sporadic. So, when I set my 2020 goals, I decided to put some actual numbers around it. I wanted some consistency with my running. I decided I would run 100 five-kilometer runs in 2020. Some would be official races because I just love official races. I love the bling and the t-shirts and the excitement of the crowd as we run through the streets. Race days are my favorite. I knew I wouldn't be able to do 100 official five-kilometer events so I made the goal just to run the runs. Some would be outside with friends. Some would be outside alone at the park. Some would be in my basement on the treadmill. Each run would be at least 3.13 miles. I would do that 100 times in the year 2020.

As big as that goal was, it wasn't big enough. I had it mapped out from the start. I knew that I had to average two runs per week and that would knock the goal out. I don't love running in the cold, but I can run outside all the way down to twenty-eight degrees. I only say that because that's the coldest I've ever run in. Who knows what I could actually do. Of course, I ended up crushing the goal because it was "doable" from the start. I decided to stick with the original goal, but

I did add in a few things to challenge myself along the way. I added in several longer runs in the form of ten-kilometer runs. And I even completed a half-marathon. What? I know! That wasn't even on my radar as a goal so that was a nice surprise. I knew I wanted to really push myself, so when the opportunity came up, I jumped on it.

I have friends who set "stretch" goals. It's an interesting concept of setting one main goal and then adding on a more aggressive, larger goal in that same category. This means the main goal of $10,000 in our example would be the main goal and the $15,000 would be considered the stretch goal. I've never tried it, but I can see how it might be beneficial. I like to keep things super simple, so I stick with just one goal.

I've gotten in the habit now of writing every goal I can think of down on paper. Then I make sure I go back and ask myself, "Do you REALLY want it?" If the answer is yes, then I take it a step further and make myself explain WHY I want it. I've stopped playing around with my goals. I have seen and felt the incredible power of writing goals down and then actually achieving them. It's the most incredible experience ever. So, I make sure I am only focusing and spending time on goals I really want to achieve. Fluff might be ok in other parts of our lives, but no fluff is allowed in our goals! Deal?

The point is, there are so many wonderful ways to set goals. You can use my system or create one that works for you. Just pick one and give it a go. You will never know just how far you can push yourself until your goals start to get a little scary. Like running-a-half-marathon-with-two-weeks'-advance-notice-and-no-training scary. I highly recommend it!

Need help with some MASSIVE goal setting? Getting your priorities straight is the first step. Visit www.TheLadyCEObook.com and watch the video titled **The gift of clarity on your priorities.**

Is it your dream or someone else's?

As I've already mentioned, sometimes I still let myself write down goals that I don't really want to accomplish. It doesn't happen as much as before but it still happens. I know so many people who get caught in that trap. It can start from a very young age. Our parents have dreams for us, which isn't a bad thing. Until we have our own dreams, we need to be pushed in a certain direction. That fits in nicely with my philosophy about it being ok to not know what you want. Even if you take steps towards a dream someone else has for you and you decide it's not what you want, there is still so much power in knowing what you don't want.

When I first started my insurance agency way back when, I had really big hopes and dreams for it. As I mentioned before, I fell into the trap of "bigger is better." I had visions of a big office and lots of employees and staff with lots of space. So, I started down that path. Every few years, I would hire some new people because I wanted my company to grow. I would hire support staff and I would hire sales staff. The only problem was that I wasn't very good at hiring and firing. Unfortunately, I had to get good at firing, but it comes with the territory, I guess.

My business was growing, for sure, but I didn't have a clear vision of how I wanted everything to work and run. After a few years, I was asked to be a part of something called The Circle of Excellence. It was a small, handpicked group of Independent Insurance Agency owners that met certain criteria. We would meet once a quarter to discuss how to run better agencies and how to be better businesspeople.

I was honored and thrilled to be a part of this group of business owners who represented some top insurance agencies in the Midwest. I knew I could learn so much from them. I also knew I had a lot to offer if anyone needed help with their social media or learning how to generate massive amounts of referrals for their business. That was kind of my thing, even early on. At this point in my agency, I hadn't quite come to grips with the fact that what I thought I wanted wasn't really what I wanted. I was still in the mindset of "build your company as big as you can get it."

I knew from the start that I didn't fit into insurance as a typical insurance agent or agency owner. Being invited to be a part of The Circle of Excellence helped me see that even more clearly. I started to compare myself and my agency to the others in the group. That's a recipe for disaster right there. I would look at agencies that were the same size as mine and do the comparison game. I would look at agencies bigger than mine and do the comparison game. Just a heads up – that is always a game you will lose.

One day, my husband pointed something out to me. After hearing me talk about some of the agencies, he said, "What's their profit?"

"Umm… what?"

One agency I mentioned that was the same size production-wise had twice as many employees, which meant much higher payroll than we had. Another agency that was twice as big as ours had three partners, which meant all profits were split at least three ways.

Huh… that was an interesting question. I had never thought about it like that before. That was one of the things that helped me get clarity on "bigger is not better." It's more about how much the profits are and what my quality of life is like by being a business owner and not just an insurance agent.

In mid-2019, there was another goal that kept popping up for me that wasn't really something I was clear on. It was related to a program called 75 Hard. If you haven't heard of it, you should Google it right away. It's something truly spectacular. I knew a few people that had completed it or were attempting to, and I thought it would be the best thing in the world to do for myself.

Let's pause for a minute so I can explain to you exactly what the program is. Most people confuse it with a fitness challenge. While there are some fitness aspects to it, there is so much more to it than that. For seventy-five days, with no rest days or breaks, you have to do certain things:

Follow a diet of any kind. You pick the eating plan you want but you have to stick to it. No cheating and no alcohol.

A forty-five-minute outdoor workout. Yep. It gets cold in Kansas where I live but that doesn't matter – those are the rules.

A forty-five-minute indoor workout.

Drink one gallon of water.

Read ten pages of a book. No Audible stuff allowed here; you have to actually read the words on the page.

Take a progress picture of yourself.

All of that. Every. Single. Day. For seventy-five days straight. Does that sound awesome or terrible? When I first heard about the program, I thought it was the most insane thing I had ever heard. I thought there was no way I could ever do that. But the more I heard about it, the more curious, but still terrified, I was about the program. Eventually, I decided to jump on the bandwagon and give it a go. I was all-in! Or so I thought. For me, it wasn't a fitness challenge; it was a no-bullshit challenge.

After admiring the program from afar for over a year, I decided to give it a go! And... I failed. Really badly and really early. The first time, I only got through a few days. Then the self-deprecating thoughts crept in, and I basically gave up on myself. With something like this, you aren't really disappointing others because this program isn't for others. It's for you, and I basically gave up on me and stopped. I don't remember how long it was until I attempted the program a second time. Again, I decided to take the flying leap, and I flung myself forward into the program. Only to fail AGAIN the second time a few days in. Jesus take the wheel – what was the matter with me!

The matter was that the motivation just wasn't there. Yet. I wasn't tired enough of my excuses. I wasn't sick enough of how I half-assed some parts of my life. I'm not saying my life was bad, by any means. I was living an incredible life, but I wasn't living up to my potential. I wasn't living full-out like I knew I should. I was letting excuses and busyness rule my schedule and control how I lived my life. And then COVID hit. It wiped everything off my schedule. It took away all of my excuses and left me with a clear picture of what was important and who was important. It left me with a lot of time that I didn't give myself previously. So I decided to give it another go.

Stop looking back. You aren't going that way.

We all know people who live in the past. They want to talk about the "good old days" or the "glory days." It makes me sad when I hear people going on and on about previous accomplishments like nothing great is ever going to happen again. Too often people are turned around looking backwards so much that they end up going that way.

Of course, your past is important. It's a part of who you are, and there are some incredible lessons we can learn from our past failures and past wins. The problem is when you get so focused on history that you can't keep moving forward with the future. We get stuck in the past in both good memories and bad memories.

had no idea just how much I craved carbohydrates and sugar. I'm not talking about pasta and bread carbohydrates. I am talking about brownies, cookies, cake, and ice cream. I had gotten lazy and complacent and let those foods become everyday foods. Just FYI, ice cream is a sometimes food, so don't kid yourself on that. When I cut those things out of my diet, I went through withdrawal. Badly.

Going through sugar withdrawal easily derailed me the first two times. But not this last time. My mind was right, and my excuses faded away. I hung in there and leveled-up every area of my life. I was able to show myself what was possible and also show those around me what was possible. When I started moving my body more, my family moved their bodies more. When I cleaned up the way I ate, my family cleaned up the way they ate. When I cut the bullshit out of my life, so did those around me.

It was a beautiful ripple effect that I didn't see coming. It's an incredible experience. I suggest you give it a go.

Why did I keep trying even though I failed so many times? Because I knew I could do it. I truly believed in my heart that I could do it. I knew that if I could just get myself in the right state with motivation and disgust, that I could lean in and find the determination I needed inside. I've seen this before in my life. I've seen myself get so sick and tired of my current situation that I completely change everything.

In my business, I eat a lot. That sounds a little weird but it's true. I have lots of lunches out with friends and referral partners. I host private lunches and special events. It seems like there is always food around. That's one thing I struggle with. COVID gave me the gift of no more lunches and social gatherings around food. It took all of that away so that temptation wasn't something I had to deal with. I just didn't have the confidence in myself that I could go to my favorite restaurants and make excellent food choices. I had tried too many times and failed. This time, the excuse was gone. It was completely removed from my life.

I am not saying this program was easy. It's not. It's truly a beast and not something to be taken lightly. But having the food temptation removed gave me the extra confidence to try again. It gave me the extra push to give it one more try. Guess what? I did it! I absolutely did it, and it was such an incredible gift to myself. I struggled every single day to get the tasks in that needed to be done. I fought every day to check the boxes and move with integrity. My body hurt every night when I went to bed and then again, every morning when I woke up. It seemed like I couldn't ever get through a project without having to go to the bathroom because I was drinking so much water. I had to be so careful what I put on my schedule because I had to make time for the two workouts each day.

It sucked every single day. It was the best gift I have ever given myself. The clarity I got about my habits and about myself has changed me forever. The biggest realization occurred when I came face to face with some serious food addictions. I

In my opinion, people are too scared to pivot or to change so they hang on to the memory of incredible past glory days they have created in their minds. They often forget that the reality behind the memory wasn't as amazing as they think it was or they are fuzzing over the details of the hard work or dedication that it took to get them there.

On Christmas Day 2020, I watched an incredible documentary on Amazon with my husband. It was the story of the Bee Gees called *How Can You Mend a Broken Heart*. Yes, those Bee Gees. Yes, I know I wasn't even born during the height of their success. If you haven't seen it, put it on your list of things to do right away. Most people recognize that the Bee Gees had an incredibly successful career in music, but, of course, there is so much that the world doesn't know.

Most people know them as a popular disco band from the late seventies. But they actually started as a band in 1958. YES! Isn't that incredible? They had their first rise in the early sixties along with The

Beatles. The band was made up of three brothers. When their success in the sixties started to fizzle, the band broke up. They dissolved the band and went their separate ways.

After a few years, they got the band back together. The documentary explains that when they came back together, they appreciated and respected each other much more. The band was actually much stronger because they had gone their separate ways and decided to come back stronger. They started to produce some incredible hits as an R&B band. These three men had so much talent and the voices of angels. They had their ups and down and their struggles, but they stayed with it and kept working through different sounds and evolving.

When the band came back together, their sound had changed. Their sound had evolved into something different. Instead of hanging onto the way it used to be, they rolled with it and worked with different music studios and producers to help develop the new songs. They didn't dig their heels in to a specific genre or identity. They went where the music took them. The three brothers not only had beautiful voices, they wrote their own songs. And what incredible songs they were!

Something pretty incredible happened during the late seventies. They got a call and were asked to come up with some songs for what would end up being *Saturday Night Fever*. At this point, they were a band writing and singing their own songs. They had never written anything like a soundtrack before. They hadn't written any songs for a specific purpose or a specific person. They just wrote and sang about what moved them. This was a new experience for them. If my count is correct, this was about the third time in their music career that they had to pivot or move in a new direction. They had to be open to entering new and uncharted territory to see if the opportunity was a good fit for them.

Needless to say, it paid off big time, and because of *Saturday Night Fever*, they had more songs on top of the charts than any other artist in history. The *Saturday Night Fever* record went on to sell a bazillion copies! Ok, a bazillion is an exaggeration but not by much. That record shattered previous record sales and took its place in history. But then... Yikes! I won't spoil the story for you because I really hope you will watch it. The documentary is done in a non-political way and it tells such a beautiful story and takes you on a journey that has its ups and downs but isn't overly dramatic and isn't trying to create an agenda.

I will tell you that, due to no fault of their own, the Bee Gees basically get attacked and dragged down. Literally at the top of their career, just living their lives and spreading joy with their music, they get attacked and their careers are dragged down. It's heartbreaking when you hear what happens to these three brothers who are at the top of their games.

After several years of mental and physical struggle, the brothers got a call that would offer them an opportunity to change everything. There was one condition... It was a direction they had not gone in before. It was something they had never done before. They had to decide if they would take that chance and once again reinvent themselves in their music career. Luckily, they said yes and continued to change the music world with their talents.

I am telling you, that documentary is so beautifully done, and it moved my heart. It honestly changed the way I thought about a few things. It moved me emotionally and opened my eyes to a few things in my own world that I need to work on.

Here's where I am going with this. Change can be scary. Man, it can be so scary! Especially when it's not you wanting to make the change. The Bee Gees were forced several times to make a change. They had choices, of course, but, ultimately, they decided to make certain pivots and changes to keep their lives and careers moving forward. You read about how much I struggled with changing my identity when I left real estate.

I want you to be open to new things. I want you to be open to doors that God and the universe will open for you. For me, and at one point for the Bee Gees, it was more like a swift kick in the ass, but it was a door that needed to be walked through.

Stay open to the idea that your best days are actually in front of you. Stay open to the idea that so much greatness is still coming your way.

Are you really injured or are you just hurt?

The best thing I've ever done for myself is to become a runner. For the last four or five years, I would run a little here and there, but I never thought of myself as a runner. I would even tell jokes about how the only time I would actually run was if a bear was chasing me. I was never consistent with it. One thing I recognize about myself is I'm always on the lookout for things I want to accomplish or add to my "let's try that" list.

I've admired runners for a long time. I love that you have to be both mentally and physically strong to do it. Whenever I see someone doing something amazing or accomplishing something, I always think,

"Oh, good for them!" but then I wait to see if I feel any envy. Even just the slightest bit of "I wish I could do that" or "I wish I could have that in my life," then I know I need to add it to my accomplishment list. The secret formula for me is encouragement mixed with a bit of envy. In this case, I use envy as a tool, and I don't see it as a bad thing.

That's how I started my journey to being a runner a few years ago. Plus, I knew it would be a great excuse to buy cute running shoes and running clothes. Don't mind me; I'm just here for the cute swag! Whatever gets you moving your body... I had been going strong for several months, and then one day, out of nowhere, I ran into a problem. On a Thursday, while I was out for a run, my foot really started hurting. It was just the one foot, and it started aching really badly around my arch area. Well, that carried into Friday, which ended up carrying into Saturday.

By Saturday, it was hurting really badly. I'm no stranger to pain. As a matter of fact, I have hurt myself plenty of times over the years with my crazy adventures and need to try new things. Not to mention that my second son was born with no anesthesia. Yep, no pain meds for me! And not on purpose, but we will save that story for another day.

I finally surrendered to the fact that I probably hurt my foot. I decided to take Sunday off from running to give it a day to heal up a little. Come Monday afternoon, I had to get back at it. I was working out at Orange Theory and it was a challenge day. That day's challenge was to see how fast you can run two miles. Well, you know I can't back down from that! I can't let a little thing like a tweaked foot slow me down on challenge day.

This is probably a good time to admit that I don't always make the smartest choices when it comes to my body and injuries. I don't usually take them seriously, and I don't let the pain slow me down. It's a weird thing I have with pain. I see it as a sign that I am pushing myself and that's a good thing.

Back to the two-mile challenge at Orange Theory…

A mile into the challenge, my foot is really hurting but I figured out a way to make it not hurt so bad. When I landed on my left foot, instead of landing on my whole foot like usual, I twisted my foot to the side a little and only landed on the flat exterior part. I'm honestly lucky I didn't hurt myself doing that. Pretty quickly, I realized that was only a temporary fix.

I had just finished David Goggins' book called *Can't Hurt Me*. What an incredible foot! Fresh off that and feeling this pain, I had two things going through my mind. The first thing was "We don't stop when it hurts; we stop when we are done." I wasn't done with my challenge, so I wasn't willing to stop. The second thing was I remembered David talking about running on your toes. There's this part in the book where he talks about how the most elite runners only let the toes' bones touch the ground. They are super-fast to land and then spring right back up off the ground like they are flying through the air. That gave me an idea. I started running on my toes, and I felt like I was flying! I ran that second mile faster than I have ever run before. It was incredible. Plus, my foot didn't hurt so I knew the injury must not have been all that serious. Until I stepped off the treadmill and had to use the whole bottom of my foot to walk.

At the end of the run when I was walking a little wonky on my foot, the Orange Theory instructor comes over and asks what's up with my foot. I tell him it's been bothering me for a few days, and then I joke, "But it's not broken or anything…"

And he says back to me, "Are you sure?"

"Wait, what? Am I sure? If it was broken, I wouldn't be able to walk, right? It doesn't feel broken but I guess I've never broken my foot before so how would I know? Oh, geez."

All the rest of my workout, I'm inside my own head thinking I might have actually broken one of the bones in my foot. I'm starting to get worried because I don't want to do any damage to any bones or muscles. I surrender to the fact that I better get to the doctor to get my foot checked out. I wasn't so worried that I left without finishing my workout, though, so maybe I wasn't too worried about it, looking back.

Things got a little sketchy over the next two weeks. The first doctor I saw took x-rays and diagnosed it as broken. She said they could see shadows on the x-rays that showed trauma and a broken bone. Is it sad that I was actually a little excited that I had been running on a broken foot? See, I told you I was a little twisted when it came to things like that.

The next day, the radiologist called me just to confirm that they looked at the films of my foot and they also thought it was broken. I always appreciate a second opinion so that was fine. Both told me that I needed to see the orthopedic surgeon to confirm what needed to be done. I was supposed to stay off my foot for two weeks until I got in to see the orthopedic surgeon, but I'm sure you can imagine how I handled that. I am happy to report that I didn't do any running in those two weeks, so, technically, I did reduce my daily activities.

The best news ever came when I had the last doctor's appointment. He showed me that I have a nerve that wraps around one of the bones in my foot. Best news ever? The foot's not broken! It was the nerve that looked like a shadow in the films of my foot. No broken bones meant no cast and that meant I could keep running. My only concern was that it still hurt, and I needed to keep running. My only question for the orthopedic surgeon was "How do I stop the pain so I can keep running?" He told me that he thought I had some nerve damage but some special insoles in my shoes would give me enough support to keep running without too much pain.

That was the path I took for the next eighteen months. I continued to run on a regular basis, and I just had to put the insoles in my shoes. I ended up needing to wear them most days or my feet would ache. But I wasn't going to stop running. Had I actually broken my foot, I would have had to take a break until it healed and then would have got right back to it.

Too often, I think, people see pain as a sign of a problem. Pain can either mean a problem or progress.

Too many people stop just because there is pain. They see it as a bad thing and think it's a sign that it's time to quit.

There will be pain when you start to work on improving your body.

There will be pain when you start to clean up your diet.

There will be pain when you grow your business.

There will be pain when you improve your standards.

There will be pain as you move from one level of life to another.

You might be hurting, but you are not injured. So just keep going. I promise all of the pain is worth it. After you break through and level-up, you will feel incredible. And all of the pain will be worth it.

Could you group help you fix your biggest pain? I mean that literally. For a great video on how a member of my group fixed a major pain I was having, visit www.TheLadyCEObook.com and watch the video titled **How my Group fixed my biggest pain.**

Are you a thermostat or a thermometer?

Over the last few years, I have become very good at controlling the "temperature" around me. By temperature, I mean energy. We all have a certain energy that we put out. Others pick up on that energy. Have you ever met someone and thought to yourself, "I don't like that person"? Maybe they seemed nice enough and they didn't say or do anything wrong, you just don't care to be around that person. In my opinion, that just means your energies are not matching up. That's how I say it but maybe that's just my way of sugar-coating things, so it doesn't sound so mean.

I used to say I am the least judgmental person ever. It was like a badge of honor that I would go around saying, "Hey... I don't judge!" But that's a lie, and I have stopped saying it. We judge. We ALL judge, and that's a good thing. We make first-impression judgments all the time without even knowing we are doing it. We have to.

We have to judge if someone is friend or foe.

We have to decide if they are someone who will build us up or tear us down.

We have to decide if their standards and values are in line with ours or if they oppose ours.

We have to decide if they are going to be a good influence on us or a bad influence on us.

We have to decide if they are givers or takers.

The problem isn't in judging people; it's when you refuse to re-judge people. That's right – we must RE-judge people all the time. Let's say you meet someone, and they are having a bad day – their energy will be different than if they are having the best day ever. I prefer not to judge people on their worst day OR their best day so I am always open to re-judging those around me.

I know the word judging can have a negative connotation, so let's look at a few examples. I'm guessing you don't hang around the same people you hung around with twenty years ago. Sure, some people in your life might have been around for twenty-plus years but most of them are not.

Why is that? It's because you re-judged them. That's not a bad thing! Maybe your lives started heading in different directions. You were working on your career and they were still trying to figure out what direction they wanted to take their career. Maybe they moved to another state and it became tougher and tougher to keep in touch. Maybe your hobbies and interests no longer lined up. You were following an eating plan and working out so going to the bars until 2 a.m. no longer fit your lifestyle. Maybe your standards and values no longer lined up. That's a tough one right there but it happens and it's ok.

I have had plenty of people move on from me. For some reason, they decided I no longer fit or they decided I was not heading in the same direction as they were headed. They decided to formally end our friendship or just quietly move on from me. It sucks. It hurts. But it happens. And guess what? It's not one-sided. I have had to end friendships or move on from people also. Since I started my insurance business, I have had to be super careful who I let in my circle. Remember when I mentioned energy? In my opinion, it affects everything.

As careful as I am about letting people in, I have made mistakes. There have been times when I let takers in because I didn't see in the beginning that they brought negative energy. As crazy as this sounds, I have even had to end relationships with people who sent me business. See, I told you it would sound crazy. With some people, they think that because they send you business that they can just dump on you whenever they want. They think that just because they send you business that they can be as negative to you as they want.

In one case, I had to start telling the person my true opinion. I started trying to get them to tell me positive things with replies like, "Yes, that sucks. But tell me what you love about what you do. Tell me all the good things that happened today instead of all the bad things."

Interestingly, they started to move away from me. I would like to say that was an isolated incident. But it wasn't. There was another relationship that was much the same but even more toxic. This other person just kept using me as a punching bag, verbally. Then when I did things this person didn't like, they lashed out at me. That was terrible, so I had to just end the relationship. As much as both of these relationships helped my business, they drained my energy and drained me emotionally. After these relationships had been removed from my life, I realized just how toxic the interactions were. Cutting out negative people is always the right decision.

Even if someone helps you a lot or has helped you a lot in the past, they don't get to insult you or drag you down. They don't get to suck your energy or put you in a negative state. Pay attention to how your energy changes when you are around certain people. If your energy is always negative, it will affect everything in your life.

Negative energy will affect your health.

Negative energy will affect your family.

Negative energy will affect your goals.

Negative energy will affect your ability to accomplish your goals and to change the world. You have to protect that.

When you walk into a room, people will either say, "Oh good! Jessica is here!" or "Oh no! Jessica is here."

By controlling your energy, you get to be the thermostat in a room. You get to be the thermostat in your company. You get to be the thermostat in your family. You get to be the one that pulls others up and energizes them. People will feed off your good energy and vibes, and you will create this beautiful ripple effect all around you.

This is going to sound a little harsh. I am going to suggest you RE-judge the people in your life on a regular basis. All relationships should be mutually beneficial. If they are the only ones getting something out of it, it's not a good fit for either one of you. You bring light and energy amongst lots of other things to the relationship so don't let takers or negative people stay in your circle.

Every quarter, I like to do a little exercise with my calendar. I pull it out and look through all the appointments I had. I look at all the networking I did. I look at all the events or meetups I went to. I look at all the lunches I had. I look at all the lunches I hosted. Then I start to grade them based on how my energy was after that specific event. Did I feel drained, or did I feel energized? I give each appointment a grade. The higher my energy after the interaction, the more likely I am to do it again. The lower my energy after the interaction, the less likely I am to do it again.

The only caveats to that rule are when I teach classes, when I speak, or when I travel to meet up with my network of other business owners. I know that in the very short-term, those appointments will leave me feeling drained, only because the interactions are at a really high level and I use a lot of energy in those situations. It's a short-term drain for a long-term gain. I just came up with that. I like it!

I go through this exercise with my calendar every quarter because it's important for me to still have those feelings and interactions fresh in my mind. If I only did it every six months or once a year, I might not be able to remember the energy that I had after the meeting or lunch.

Cut the energy vampires out of your life. Be ruthless with this. In order to help others, you must protect your energy. Be selfish. Do it today.

So… What's new with you?

Are you boring? If you didn't immediately think to yourself, "No way! I'm awesome!" then the truth is that you probably are boring. I know that sounds harsh, and I have been there before. There's this terrible conversation happening on a daily basis that goes like this…

"Hey! How are you?"

"Good! How are you?"

"I'm good. What's new with you?"

"Oh, you know. Just the same old stuff. You?"

"Same here. Just the same old stuff."

It's so mind-numbing. It's painful to listen to and even more painful to be a part of.

Most of us are boring and have nothing to say, so these conversations seem normal. It's not until we brush up against someone who's interesting and adventurous that we see the glaring difference between their lives and ours. I'm going to let you in on a little secret.

People want to be around interesting people.

People want to send business to interesting people.

People want to do business with interesting people.

Just by being an interesting person and having things to talk about will set you apart in business and in life. Let's take another look at the boring conversation from before. I have about ten different replies I can give if someone asks me, "What's new with you?" I can talk about my running goals I am working on. I can talk about a new cheesecake recipe I am trying to perfect. I can talk about new marketing things I am trying in my business. I can talk about new social groups I have joined. I can talk about adventures I am planning with my husband and kids or recent ones we have just been on. I have plenty to talk about, depending on who is asking and what direction I might want to take the conversation.

But it wasn't always like this. About six years ago, I looked at my life and myself and I thought, "Dang! I am BORING!" It was an honest reflection, and I wasn't being mean or putting myself down. I just realized that I didn't have a lot going on in my life. Up until that point, it was ok. I was just fine with the way things had been going in my life. As I mentioned before, the calm and quiet that leaving real estate brought to our lives was a welcome change. Except for the short stint with the traveling trainer job, I was home for my family pretty much every night of the week. At this point, financially, we had been doing much better and the boys were getting old enough for us to be comfortable flying and traveling with them.

John and I love to travel. Before we got married, we took a ten-day trip to Europe. It was a trip of a lifetime. We visited Germany, Italy, and the United Kingdom. This was my first time traveling internationally, and, boy, was that a trip. A funny little side note here… You know how once couples reach a certain point in their relationship, they go for a weekend away or something like that? Not us. The first overnight trip we ever decided to take together was a ten-day exploration through Europe. I'm pleased to announce that our relationship survived.

We didn't stay landlocked for the first five years of our sons' lives because we don't like to travel; we just didn't want to take the littles on trips. Add to that the fact that John refuses to leave his bear cubs. When the boys were about two and three, I convinced him to take a weekend trip to California to visit some friends. He did ok but was nervous about being away from the boys the whole time. I still can't get him to leave the boys behind to take trips.

That's ok. That's one of the main reasons he is such a great father.

My realization that I was boring came right around the same time that we became comfortable with traveling with the boys. Thank goodness! Once we started traveling and seeking adventure, we didn't stop! We went to the beach. We went skiing. We went to the lake. And we started looking for adventure in our own city, which we had overlooked for many years. Once we made the decision, it quickly became a lifestyle.

But I didn't just stop with my family. I started working on being personally interesting also. I started reading more and started taking online classes. Most of the online classes and courses I took had to do with business or personal development. I know they might not sound appealing to some people, but these subjects are fascinating to me. I started to go on personal adventures. I explored different places with friends and by myself. I had no idea the incredible journey I had set myself on. I still remember looking at myself and seeing a middle-aged mom who lived in the middle of the United States that sold insurance. Nothing interesting about any of that. Until I decided to change it and change the way I looked at myself.

Is it easy being adventurous? No. However, most things in life are not easy. Planning trips can be time-consuming. Luckily, my husband is very good at it. I can point him in the direction of an adventure I want us to go on and he is great at planning the traveling part of it. It's not easy packing up the family and heading out into the unknown. It's also not easy sitting on the couch watching TV and eating potato chips knowing you could be doing so much more with your life.

An added bonus is that each adventure comes with special memories, interesting conversation, and unplanned lessons. About half of the adventures, we go on don't turn out as planned. In December of 2019, we had the incredible experience of going on a Disney cruise. As much amazingness as we experienced on that trip, like a free room upgrade to a suite and finding the best candy shop hidden in the ship, not everything went as planned.

One day, our adventure was swimming with the dolphins in Atlantis and my boys had the best time. The next day, we headed out to feed the stingrays on Disney's private island. Let's just say that was NOT the best adventure ever. About twenty minutes into that, my youngest son got bit and went running from the water yelling. My other son got freaked out, so he took off also. That left John and me chasing after two yelling kids in a sea of families having a great time. Yes, we were THAT family!

After we got the boys calmed down, I reminded them that not every adventure is the best adventure. They have heard that so many times that they get it. I reminded them what a great experience we had the day before with the dolphins. I reminded them that we have no idea what's going to happen on each adventure and that's why we keep going. Then I told them this was going to make a GREAT story one day! They laughed at that because they get it when it comes to trying new things.

I want you to challenge yourself to try something new each month. I know it can be scary and maybe it sounds hard. I am not talking about standup paddle boarding or zip lining or anything way outside of your comfort zone – although I did try both of those this past year and fully intend to keep doing them both. Start small if you have to. Start trying one new restaurant a month. Try to make one new recipe at home once a month. Go to one new museum a month. Read one new book a month. Learn one new skill a month. I promise it will be worth it. Let me know how it goes. Just remember, if it turns out terrible, THAT also makes a great story.

How do I become a leader and develop a team?

I have the incredible pleasure of being friends with a lot of business owners and self-employed individuals. I am also connected with a large number of business owners and self-employed individuals on social media. Because of that, I get random questions that pop into my instant messages. My favorites are: "How do I fire someone?" or "How do I know if I should fire someone?" Those make me laugh a little because they insinuate that I am good at firing people. Unfortunately, I have had to fire a lot of people, so I actually am good at it.

My favorite question to answer or have a conversation around is: "How do I build a team?" I love this question because it tells me the person asking the question is starting to think like a business owner and not just a self-employed person. It's a step a lot of self-employed entrepreneurs and small-business owners never get to. As ambitious and inventive as we can be, we can be so short-sighted at times.

What do I mean by that? A lot of entrepreneurs and small-business owners are the perfect example of "can't see the forest for the trees." I say "we" because I have been there and worked through all of this on my own. We have a big dream or an idea to start. In all of our inventiveness, we run out and make it happen. The only issue is that we don't see our new venture as a business; we see it as a job.

Let's take a look at the traditional solopreneur. I'll take you down the path of an insurance agent because it's the easiest for me to explain. But this can be applied to just about any business.

In the beginning, it's all fun and exciting. The hope and dreams keep you going and grinding forward. You are working on bringing in the leads and referrals. Guess what? You did a great job and now you have some potential clients who are interested in working with you. You get some insurance quotes sent off for them to review. Things are going great, and this goes on for several months. You are bringing in new business and growing your business.

After just a few months, the tasks really start to add up. You are bringing in new business, quoting and closing new business, issuing new insurance policies, collecting the signed applications for those policies, sending out new auto insurance ID cards to the clients, sending new evidence of insurance to mortgage companies so the premiums can get paid, answering client calls with billing questions, working with the clients and underwriting about issues that come up when the insurance company sends someone out to inspect the house that has a new policy, helping clients file claims, following up on claims and working with clients on how their policies actually work... And you are the only person showing up to handle all of this every day.

That was insurance specific but I think you get the picture. Even from the very start, we look at it like we are the ones that have to handle everything. My questions to you are: "How long do you think you can keep that up? How long do you want to keep that up?" I don't know about you, but I'm not trying to spend the rest of my life working from 9 a.m. until 5 p.m. every day. My hunch is that, at some point, you are going to get burnt out. Remember how we already talked about that? And what kind of client experience do you think that is? If you get tired and don't show up to do the work, no one is going to do it, which makes the situation even worse.

Let's say you are handling everything in your business, and I invite you to have lunch with me. Or you are taking a valued referral partner to lunch. We all know lunch and great conversation can easily last ninety minutes or up to two hours. I used to make fun of people who took that long at lunch until I started having lunches with interesting people that I loved spending time with. Let's say during that time, one of your clients need something. A common type of phone call insurance offices get is from clients at the department of motor vehicles. They are trying to renew their tags or tag a new car. They misplaced the evidence of insurance and need a copy of it. Now. Because they are standing in line. Do you think it's excellent customer service to make that client wait? No. That's a terrible client experience.

I'm not saying it's terrible to be a one-man show. Most of us have been there. I am just saying you can't get stuck there. Let's compare the one-man show example to a few other businesses that we consider to be professional like your doctor's office or your dentist's office. Is the doctor scheduling appointments? Is the doctor taking your temperature? Is the doctor at the front desk checking how you are after the appointment? Is your doctor calling your insurance company to see what's covered or check on payment? No. And if they did, you would think that was weird. You would get concerned because you know that's not how professional offices run.

There is an evolution and leveling-up for all businesses, but most are too afraid to keep moving. My first goal in my business was to make enough money to hire a part-time customer service person. After I did that, I hired a full-time customer service person who could help me with the paperwork that I needed for my files. At each step of the way, I never stepped away from selling. That was the very last thing I stepped away from. I considered it my personal responsibility to keep the phone ringing with new business and to keep sales coming in. Very slowly, I hired out just about everything that needed to be done so I could spend 90% of my time on money-making activities.

You want to know how to build a team? Build something that people want to be a part of. It's always very interesting to me how the first hire people want to make is salespeople. Then what? So the salespeople go out and get sales, then who is going to take care of those clients? Who's going to process those orders? Who's going to support the salespeople in general? You? I also think you have to ask yourself what kind of salesperson would take a job for a company with no support. You might be able to find and hire a few great salespeople, but you won't be able to keep them once the backend starts getting messy on their orders or with their customers.

You want to know how to be a great leader? There are thousands of books out there that will tell you how to do that. I know because I have personally read a lot about leadership. It all starts in one place. It all starts with you. You want to be a great leader and build a great team and company? First, you have to lead your own damn self. You have to create the stability in your company to support staff. You have to create the systems needed for everything to run smoothly. You have to set the tone and standards in your office. Then you have to hold the line and not budge. Great leadership starts by looking in the mirror and leading your own self.

Are you learning the lesson at each level or just using cheat codes?

I believe there are four different levels in life. Each level teaches us a lesson that we will need to master before we can move on to the next level. But there's a catch. You might understand the lesson well enough to move on, but in the next level, you have to actually apply the lesson. If you haven't mastered the lesson enough to actually apply it in the next level, you won't continue to move forward. You stay stuck until you have learned the lesson.

The first level is survival. Unfortunately, this is where most people live all of their lives. It's living paycheck to paycheck with no certainty about your future. At this level, you might know where the money is coming from but it's usually not enough to pay the bills and there is no extra to save for the future. This is the struggle bus! I spent most of my late teens and early twenties here. Just when I got caught up on my bills and got my spending under control, I would have a slow month and get right back in struggle mode. Even when I would get a little money, I wouldn't save it. I didn't know when I would have extra cash ever again so I would buy things I wanted but probably didn't need to make myself feel better. It was that exact behavior and mindset that kept me in this cycle of struggle.

If you are at the struggle level right now, the good news is that you don't have to stay there. Two simple things are keeping you at this level: habits and mindset. It's that simple. I know because I have been there before. The solution is equally simple. Spend less money while also earning more money. Why both? Because when you are stuck in struggle, one solution is not enough. Just spending less won't help much and neither will just adding more money. It has to be a combination of the two in order to get you to the next level.

Before you can move from one level to the other, you must be honest with yourself about what level you are on. I have known plenty of people in my lifetime that are in complete denial about where they are financially. You might be one of them. You might be living with mounds of credit-card debt and driving new cars while walking around pretending like everything is ok. You might be drowning in student-loan debt while renting an apartment because that student-loan payment keeps you from buying a house. If you can't be honest with yourself about where you are, I promise you will stay stuck.

I'm not saying student loans are the kiss of death so don't get caught up on that. Both my husband and I still have student loans we are paying off. At one point, I had over $40,000 in student loans and no degree. It wasn't until I was in my mid-thirties that I actually finished the degree. One day, John said to me, "We are making the payments for a degree you don't have. You are so close. You should find a way to finish it." And I did. Just be honest with yourself about the areas you need to clean up on each level.

The second level is stability. The gap from the first level to the second level is the largest because it requires the biggest mind shift out of all four levels. Going from level one to level two is so difficult because at level two there is extra money. You aren't just living paycheck to paycheck anymore. You have your monthly obligations under control and are ending the month with extra funds. The mind shift comes in having the self-discipline to take that money and do something your future self will thank you for. For some, it's saving until you reach a certain level in a savings account. After that, it's investing in retirement accounts or in other businesses.

The levels aren't just financial, of course. As you step up a level with your finances, you should also expect to step up a level or even two with your circle. When you are thinking about your financial future and saving and investing money, it's probably not a good idea to keep hanging around people who go out several nights a week and spend their cash on drinks at the bar. The circle you spent time with on the struggle bus will have to stay on the bus even when you get off. Some might come with you, but don't bet on it.

Our family was at the stability level during my early life crisis when I left real estate and moved on to other careers. My being stuck and afraid to leave one identity behind put that in jeopardy. It caused us to fall back into the survival level for a bit before we climbed back up to the stability level. That's the main reason I carried so much guilt with that part of my life. I realized that I didn't really learn the lessons from the first level and that's why I contributed to us falling backwards. In order for me to learn a lesson, it has to cost me a lot of money or it has to be extremely painful. The good news is that I definitely learned that lesson.

The third level is success. Of course, success means different things for all of us. For me, it means having more lifestyle choices. Most of what happens in my insurance agency on a daily basis has nothing to do with me. My team and I are clear on where I make the greatest impact, and we work together to make sure I stay in my lane. Because of that, I have time to work on the rest of my life.

When it comes to lifestyle levels, success offers you more options than survival or stability. Success can be where the real fun begins. You don't have to own your own business to get to this level. I stepped up to this level long before I stepped into insurance. Way back when I was in pharmaceutical sales, which seems like a lifetime ago, I stepped up to this level. I was working in a position that fit my personality very well. I was making great money and we had enough to look out for future John and Jess. I had a very relaxed schedule and was able to fit in all the mom things that I wanted to be a part of. We were taking several family vacations a year and really enjoying the trajectory we were on.

Sounds pretty nice, huh? So, then, why did I want to walk away from all of that and jump into insurance? That's a great question. At some point, I knew corporate America wasn't going to get me to the fourth level and that's "significance." I'm not saying I am there yet. I am certainly working on it. Significance for me is more about what you are doing for others than what you are doing for yourself. This book is a perfect example. I didn't write this book for me. I don't have any deep confessions I need to get off my chest to feel better. I don't need to chronicle all of this information in book form for me personally. I've lived it and learned the lessons. I have all the t-shirts, medals, selfies, and scars to prove it.

I wrote this book for you. For the mom who can't see past always having a toddler needing her and not being able to get any alone time. For the businesswoman who works her butt off but can't seem to get any traction in her life. For the wife who isn't exactly happy in her marriage but doesn't know how to fix it. For the women who feel unimpressed with themselves because they know they are living well below their capability. For anyone who feels like they don't have what it takes to do something special.

I wrote this so you could see the less-than-ideal upbringing I had. I wrote this so that I could be an example of someone who comes from nothing, had nothing, knew nothing, made tons of mistakes, and is still out here kicking and fighting her way to the top.

Look at me. Look at you. The next time you feel less than awesome, whisper to yourself, "If Jessica can do it, then I can too!"

Visit www.TheLadyCEObook.com for a special video I posted about **The ONLY reason you are not INCREDIBLE at everything**.

Conclusion.

While there is still so much left to say, I feel like this is a good place to stop. There are so many more incredible stories and lessons I want to share but we will save that for the next book.

Thank you again for coming on this journey with me. I hope you enjoyed it as much as I did.

I have built a strong business and reputation by serving others. Please let me know how I can serve you.

Interested in having me speak to your Group, Company, Team, or Organization on how to create MASSIVE amounts of Referrals? Over the last 5 years, I have generated over 3,700 Referrals. I am happy to share what I have learned and to help others apply it.

Let's connect at
www.TheLadyCEOBook.com

Made in the USA
Coppell, TX
21 April 2021

54200637R00095